Praise for
Freelancing for Newspapers

"Anyone hoping to write for the newspaper market should stop everything and read Sue Fagalde Lick's *Freelancing for Newspapers*. The chapter on generating story ideas is worth the price all by itself."

—Dale Bryant, executive editor, Silicon Valley Community Newspapers

"Sue Fagalde Lick has done a wonderful job in demystifying the world of newspaper publishing and freelancing. As Lick points out, newspapers need new material every day—and this book is a must for any writer who wants to tap into this huge, and often overlooked, market!"

—Moira Allen, editor/publisher, Writing-World.com; *Starting Your Career as a Freelance Writer*

"Sue Fagalde Lick serves up enthusiastic and informative tips and information. Lick's new book will help writers succeed in an area of freelancing that many haven't even considered."

—Angela Hoy, publisher, WritersWeekly.com

"*Freelancing for Newspapers* is an excellent text for aspiring freelancers. Sue Fagalde Lick covers all the bases in a clear journalistic style that her readers would do well to emulate."

—Marcia Preston, novelist, former editor of *Byline Magazine*

"Sue Fagalde Lick has comprehensive guide that will have seasoned and beginning writers connecting with and serving the needs of local and national newspapers as quickly as five minutes after they finish reading."

—Christina Katz, *Writer Mama: How to Raise a Writing Career Alongside Your Kids*

"This book is a must-have for any writer serious about garnering clips. Sue Fagalde Lick offers practical, hands-on advice as well as skill-building exercises geared toward both novice and experienced writers."

—Robbi Hess, editor/co-publisher *ByLine Magazine;* co-author, *Complete Idiot's Guide to 30,000 Baby Names*

Freelancing
for Newspapers

Writing for an Overlooked Market

By
Sue Fagalde Lick

Quill
Driver
Books

Sanger, California

Printed in the United States of America

Published by Quill Driver Books/Word Dancer Press, Inc.
1254 Commerce Way
Sanger, California 93657
559-876-2170 • 1-800-497-4909 • FAX 559-876-2180

QuillDriverBooks.com
Info@QuillDriverBooks.com

Quill Driver Books' titles may be purchased in quantity at special discounts
for educational, fund-raising, training, business, or promotional use.
Please contact Special Markets, Quill Driver Books/Word Dancer Press, Inc.,
at the above address, toll-free at 1-800-497-4909, or by e-mail:
Info@QuillDriverBooks.com

Quill Driver Books/Word Dancer Press, Inc. project cadre:
Doris Hall, Stephen Blake Mettee, Carlos Olivas

Quill Driver Books and colophon are trademarks of
Quill Driver Books/Word Dancer Press, Inc.

First printing

ISBN 1-884956-68-8 • 978-1884956-68-3

To order another copy of this book, please call
1-800-497-4909

Library of Congress Cataloging-in-Publication Data

Lick, Sue Fagalde.
  Freelancing for newspapers : writing for an overlooked market / by Sue Fagalde Lick.
    p. cm.
Includes bibliographical references and index.
ISBN-13: 978-1-884956-68-3 (pbk. : alk. paper)
ISBN-10: 1-884956-68-8 (pbk. : alk. paper)
1. Freelance journalism. I. Title.
PN2784.F76L53 2007
070.4'3—dc22

2007018138

For Fred, who put up with it all.

Contents

Introduction

There's Gold in That Pile of Paper

One of the best markets for freelance writing may be sitting on your kitchen table right now. I'm talking about the newspaper. In fact, if you're like me, you have a whole stack of newspapers piled on the table, on the counters, and beside your chair in the den. So do the people who could be reading your articles right now.

In the freelance writing world, newspapers are often overlooked. If you scan *The American Directory of Writer's Guidelines, Writer's Market*, and other major market guides, you will find that most of the listings are for magazine and book publishers. Yet newspapers constitute a big market for freelancers. Because there are so many newspapers and they come out so often, they require a lot of articles, usually more than the staff can provide. Freelancers fill in the gaps. They write feature stories, reviews, travel articles, profiles, and so much more.

Start looking at the newspapers that you read with an eye to freelance opportunities. Study the bylines. Staff writers are usually identified as such. Freelancers' bylines are often followed by something like "Special writer" or "Special to *The Oregonian*." Sometimes there's nothing after the name, but at the end of the article, you will see a few lines printed in italics that say something like, "Sue Fagalde Lick is a freelance writer living in South Beach, Oregon." Sometimes you see the same freelance bylines every week. These writers have managed to claim a niche in the paper for a regular gig.

Think about your work, hobbies and personal experiences. Are there subjects that you are especially interested in or knowledgeable about? You can turn this interest and knowledge into articles for your town's daily or weekly newspaper. Specialized newspapers for antique collectors, fishermen, bridge players, and just about any group you can think of offer other outlets for your writing. Your church, your lodge, and the industry in which you work probably all publish local, statewide or national newspapers. These are also places where you could sell freelance articles.

In the pages that follow, we will look at these opportunities in depth.

This book was born out of my Freelancing for Newspapers and Opinionated Writing classes, which I still teach online and at various workshops. It felt like time to put all the information in one convenient place. Each chapter explores an aspect of the newspaper freelance business, followed by activities to use to put the information into action.

This book should help you begin, but neither this book nor the others I will recommend are enough to get you published in the newspapers. To write for newspapers, you must read newspapers. The more of a news junky you are, the better. Read newspapers cover to cover, looking for story ideas and freelance opportunities and getting a feel for newspaper style. Read every section—sports, business, food, science, religion, news, whatever. Grab the free newspapers you find at libraries, stores and restaurants and the ones that come in the mail to you and to other family members. Those that don't seem to use freelance are still valuable as sources of article ideas.

Maybe you prefer other types of writing and never thought of yourself as a newspaper writer. There was a time when I didn't care much about newspapers either. Back in high school when I was choosing a career, I wanted to write poetry and short stories. However, knowing I needed to earn a living, I decided I would learn to write for magazines. When I arrived at San Jose State University for orientation, I discovered that the magazine major had just been eliminated. All of us would-be *Atlantic Monthly* editors had been transferred into "reporting and editing." Apparently God knows what he's doing. I found that I enjoyed newspaper writing and I was good at it.

I earned my bachelor's degree in journalism at San Jose State and started my career as an intern at the *Milpitas Post*, one of a chain of weekly newspapers in the San Jose area. In the years that followed, I spent nearly thirty years working as a staff writer, editor and photographer on various newspapers in California and Oregon. I also freelanced. A lot. I was a regular contributor to *Bay Area Parent, San Jose Mercury News, High Technology Careers, Portuguese Heritage Journal, South Valley Times,* and other papers. Eventually, I had enough freelance work to quit my regular job.

In recent years, I have rekindled an old interest in writing poetry and fiction and earned a master of fine arts degree in creative writing from Antioch University, Los Angeles, but I still feel most at home in what my grandfather used to call "the funny papers." In fact, I recently became the "baby boomer correspondent" for *Northwest Senior News.* Once you get hooked on newspapers, it's hard to stay away.

Certainly in these days of CNN, online news, and cell phones that can access the Internet, you may wonder if newspapers are going out of style. They aren't. They are adapting, just as they always have. Knowing that the electronic media will always scoop them with the headlines, they are offering more depth and variety, the stories that can't be told in a two-minute news bite. They are also expanding into the Internet and other media.

Back in the 1800s, it could take a month to receive any kind of news from home. Long before that, people nailed pages to the sides of buildings. News comes faster all the time, and the way it is transmitted will continue to change. Although this book focuses on print newspapers, what you read here can also be used for the ever-growing list of online publications. In fact, most major newspapers already publish much of their content on the Internet as well as on paper. Many offer additional "bonus" stories on their websites. So the skills you learn here will be useful, no matter what happens as technology advances.

Take another look at that pile of newspapers on your kitchen table. See how many articles there are? Well, tomorrow, next week, or next month, other issues will arrive full of more stories. And that's where you come in.

Chapter 1

Newspapers as a Freelance Market

Any writer who is serious about writing, selling and communicating with readers should consider newspapers as a possible market. Here's why:

Most people read at least one newspaper regularly. Even people who don't read many magazines or books will look at a newspaper. If you want to prove this to yourself, try writing something controversial for your daily paper and include your e-mail address. When I wrote an editorial about airport security for *The Oregonian*, my e-mail inbox was flooded with comments, both positive and negative. About half the readers thanked me for expressing what they had been feeling while the other half invited me to leave the country.

When I write opinion pieces for our local paper, people telephone, e-mail and stop me on the street to tell me they read and liked my piece. No one except the people involved ever said anything about the articles I wrote almost every month for several years for *Oregon Business Magazine*, although those took a lot more work.

In the United States, we have approximately 1,500 daily newspapers. Among those, the National Newspaper Association reports that four, the *Wall Street Journal*, *USA Today*, *New York Times* and *Los Angeles Times*, attract well over 1 million readers each, and many other dailies are read by more than 500,000 people. According to the NAA, nearly eight in ten American adults in the top fifty U.S. markets read a daily newspaper every weekday, and more than six in ten read one each Sunday. Nationally, more than 54 million newspapers are sold daily, with an average of 2.3 readers per copy. On Sundays, that goes up to 58 million with an average of 2.4 readers per copy. Compare that to recent studies that show fewer than half of American adults have read a book within the last year.

Most communities have at least one weekly newspaper; some have several. With countless special interest newspapers and hundreds of English-language newspapers published outside the United States, writing for newspapers is a great way to maximize your audience.

Longtime freelancer Sally Abrahms says she writes mostly for magazines these days, but if she wanted everyone in Boston to see her story, she'd sell it to the *Boston Globe* newspaper because everybody reads it.

You have more of a chance of becoming a household name via the newspaper than you do from a hundred magazine articles. If you fear the Internet is taking over, note that more and more newspapers publish their articles online, but they also continue to publish on paper.

The newspaper market is far bigger than most people think. It's not just the large metropolitan dailies and community weeklies. Go out for coffee, and you'll probably see a table or rack full of newspapers. Gays, Hispanics, coffee lovers, vegetarians, parents, teens, seniors, veterans, dog lovers—every group you can think of has a newspaper. Visit an antiques store, and you'll find several newspapers on antiques. Most religions have local, regional and national publications. And don't overlook newspapers aimed at particular industries, such as *Computer World, Hotel & Motel Management,* or the many publications for educators, lawyers, Teamsters and other workers. For every career, there seems to be a newspaper.

Newspapers come out more often, and there are more of them, so they require more editorial content. At daily and weekly general-interest papers, staff writers cover most of the news and many of the main features. The Associated Press and other wire services provide national and world news. But there are many stories the staff and wire services don't cover. That's where freelancers come in. Smaller newspapers are always understaffed. I have worked for community papers where the editorial staff consisted of one editor and a part-time college intern. How did they survive? Freelance writers.

Tucson Weekly editor Jimmy Boegle says he has four full-time editorial employees and about twenty-five writers who freelance for him regularly. "As a matter of fact, about three-quarters of our stuff is done by freelancers."

Freelancers offer advantages to newspaper editors: They bring a fresh point of view, they can take on temporary or special assignments, and they only have to be paid for the work they do. No benefits, no down time. "When newspaper companies start looking at the bottom line, they like freelancers a lot," says Dale Bryant, executive editor of the Silicon Valley Community Newspapers chain.

And newspapers are a good place to break in. "It's always going to be easier to crack a newspaper than a magazine," says Brett Harvey, former executive director of the American Society of Journalists and Authors. Because they come out more often and have more space to fill, newspapers need more writers.

"The smaller, community-based publications are more open to untested writers and, although they're less visible and lower-paying, there's much more opportunity for you as a writer to play the field a little bit and try things," says David L. Ulin, book editor for the *Los Angeles Times*. He says he learned the newspaper business working as a freelancer and eventually an editor for the *Los Angeles Reader*. "That was my graduate school education. I got to write a lot of different kinds of different pieces, things that no one would let me write. I got to review movies, I got to write news stories, I got to edit pieces, I got to be involved in cover choices and writing cover copy and teasers and all. I really got to learn how it all got put together."

How Do Magazine and Newspaper Writing Differ?

Newspapers aren't as pretty as magazines. Printed on grayish newsprint instead of slick white paper, the front page will probably be a conglomeration of articles. On the inside pages, your stories are more likely to share space with advertisements. Newspapers are put together in a rush, so you may see more typographical errors. Overall, content counts more than appearance.

Many of the tasks involved in writing for newspapers and magazines are the same. If you have written for magazines, some of what follows will seem familiar. There are similarities and differences:

• **Mission.** Every newspaper and magazine has a mission. To succeed, you need to make sure your stories fit that mission. For many general-interest daily and weekly newspapers, the mission is to be *the* place readers look for news and features about the area in which they live and work. Remember the real estate slogan "location, location, location"? For community newspapers, change that to "local, local, local." If there is no local angle, they can't use it, no matter how fascinating or well-written it might be.

Thus your feature on a nuclear power plant in Minnesota will not get published in Dallas—unless you can find a local angle. Can you tie in the problems or successes of the Minnesota plant with something that's happening in Dallas? Is a similar plant about to be built there? Now you have a local angle. Is a guy from Texas running the plant in Minnesota? Bingo.

The Newport *News-Times*, where I worked for a while, calls itself "The information source for the Central Oregon Coast." They have it printed on a big banner in the conference room, they put it at the top of the front page of every issue, and it's printed on their stationery. If it doesn't happen on the Central Oregon Coast, they don't want to know about it, but if a reporter can find a local angle, they're interested. A good example is tsunamis. The *News-Times* has run countless articles on tsunamis since the big one hit Indonesia in January 2005. God willing, we may never have a tsunami here, but everyone is worried about being prepared in case the big wave comes.

Other papers center on a particular group or interest rather than a location. The newspaper put out by the Catholic Archdiocese of Chicago may run some wire service stories about Catholics outside of Chicago, but it won't be running anything about Methodists. I used to work for an Hispanic newspaper called *El Observador*. If the story did not have a connection to the Hispanic community, it did not get in. I also wrote several articles for *High Technology Careers*. I'm not a techie, but I sold them personality profiles of people working in Silicon Valley. One of my favorite pieces was on how not to let a foreign accent keep you from getting ahead. I resold it later to *Toastmaster* magazine with only minor changes, but for the *High Technology Careers* audience, I interviewed people in the computer industry and focused on their problems.

Another story that got refocused and resold was on bees. I'm petrified of bees, always have been. My original query went to *Bay Area Parent*, which bought a story on how to keep kids from getting stung without making them unreasonably fearful of bees. I used most of the same information in an article for the *San Jose Mercury News* on how to work in the garden without getting stung. I reslanted that story again for a camping magazine, explaining how to keep bees from spoiling your camping trip.

Figure out the newspaper's mission and send stories that fit. If they don't fit, they will never get in. "There's a sense on the part of young writers, and I had it when I was starting out, that if your work is good enough or interesting enough or brilliant enough that they'll buy it no matter what, and that's not true," David L. Ulin says.

• **News peg.** Timeliness is often a factor in getting an article published in the newspaper. Magazines frequently buy "evergreens," stories that can run at any time, but newspaper editors will ask, "Why publish this story now?" A feature on an artist is more likely to sell if it can be tied to an upcoming gallery show. A school program may be deemed worthy of a feature if it's new, being considered for budget cuts, or just won an award. A local athlete preparing for an upcoming triathlon is a good bet. Stories that can be tied to holidays or anniversaries of major events have a better chance of getting published.

Stories on chocolate sell for Valentine's Day, religious stories abound as Easter approaches, and skiing sells in January. In late August, the newspapers will be full of back-to-school stories. In September, they will run articles about the anniversary of the 9/11 terrorist attacks on New York and Washington and look back at the double whammy of hurricanes Katrina and Rita.

• **Lead times.** Newspapers don't work as far ahead as magazines. Most magazines are put together at least two months in advance. Some editors work as much as a year ahead. For daily newspapers, the news and sports sections are written, edited and laid out less than twenty-four hours before publication. Feature sections are planned a little farther ahead. This may be a few days, a week or, in the case of holidays or other special events, a month or two. For weekly newspapers, you have two weeks at the most. Monthlies work about a month ahead.

Staff writers quickly learn that there's no room for writer's block in the newspaper business. Whether you feel like writing or not, you sit down and write the story. Freelancers with the same work ethic will move to the top of the editor's list. "If you can do a quick turnaround, you can get more work," says Sue Harrison, arts editor of Massachusetts' *Provincetown Banner.* "If a story falls through on Wednesday and I call you on Thursday and you can give me 500 words by 5 P.M. Friday, that's a good thing and encourages me to call you."

• **Approaching the editor.** How one pitches a story idea to a newspaper editor is also different. Many writers complain that they mail their queries to newspaper editors and never get a response. Unfortunately, that's not unusual. As a former newspaper editor, I understand how quickly an editor gets buried. The pace is perpetually frantic. All she can do is fight the closest fire and let the rest pile up. Information is coming at the editor via telephone, fax, mail, and e-mail in a constant deluge. At the same time, the editor is trying to write, edit stories, lay out pages, and supervise the staff. There simply isn't time to deal with a lot of written correspondence.

How do you get through to the editor? Unless their guidelines tell you otherwise, submit by e-mail. Although writers are still being taught to submit book proposals and magazine submissions on paper, today most newspaper editors prefer e-mail for pitches, article submissions, and nearly all communication. A few still prefer snail mail queries, but most editors don't want to deal with paper. Everything travels over the Internet.

Many writers maintain that it's all right to telephone a newspaper editor with story ideas, but ultimately the editor will have to see something in writing—which he would like you to send by e-mail.

• **Pay.** You may have heard that newspapers don't pay as well as magazines. In many cases, that's true. They usually pay better than literary magazines do for poetry or fiction, but that's not saying much. I have seen local newspapers—recently—that paid less than a penny a word. If you do the math, a 1,000-word article would net you less than $10. Surely it would take you at least two hours to research and write it, probably longer. Five to ten cents a word is more common for community weeklies, which still doesn't make you rich. But these are acceptable markets if you need experience and clips more than you need cash.

There are other papers that pay real money. The big dailies generally pay at least $100 for columns and opinion pieces, more for feature articles. The *Chicago Tribune* pays up to $500 for travel pieces. The *Christian Science Monitor* starts at $200 an article. Rates at the *Los*

Angeles Times range from $250 to $600, depending on what section they run in. Whatever you make from one publication may not be all you can earn from that piece. Often an article can be resold to a non-competing publication or reslanted for a paper going to a different audience, as I did with the bee story.

• **Writing style.** Traditionally, newspaper articles have been written in what is called the "inverted pyramid" style. You start with the most important information and work your way down to the least important so that if the story is too long for the space available, the editor can cut it off from the bottom. Such cutting still happens. How many times have you read an article and felt that something was missing? It probably got shortened at the last minute.

If you wind up writing news stories covering events, government meetings or press conferences, you will still need to employ the inverted pyramid. People want the most important facts first in that type of article. Front-page news articles usually jump to an inside page, but how many readers will actually turn the page for the rest of the story? You can't count on them reading a key piece of information buried at the end of the story.

As a freelancer, you are more likely to be assigned to write feature articles (non-news), which are written more like magazine articles. You will have a lead, some background, development of the story and a conclusion. You might find yourself with less space than you would like, and you may be asked to focus on one aspect of a subject rather than a broad view, but you can be relatively confident that your story will run intact and readers will read most if not all of it.

Another aspect of newspaper writing which falls under the heading of style relates to how newspapers handle details such as punctuation, capitalization, dates, addresses and abbreviations. In general, the writing is more casual

and more streamlined than you see in books and magazines. Most newspapers use the *Associated Press Stylebook*
as a guide. Buy a copy if you want to write much for
newspapers. The editor will bless you if she doesn't have
to change every date from "1 February 2003" to "Feb. 1,
2003" or times from "two o'clock" to "2 P.M."

How Do You Find Newspaper Freelance Openings?

Now the fun begins. Gather up all the newspapers you can find at
your house, including the ones your parents, spouse, siblings, children
or roommates receive. Set aside all the ones that don't interest you at
all, because you don't want to write for a publication you don't want to
read. Trust me. Now start reading. Go for the big local daily first. If
you don't subscribe, buy one out of a newsstand.

Once you finish the papers at your house, go to the library. You'll
find newspapers you didn't know existed.

Go beyond the books to the periodicals department. You will
probably see lots of magazines. But off to the side somewhere, you'll
find the newspapers. They may be stacked on shelves, hanging from
poles or piled on a table. They may be a few days or weeks or even
months old. That's okay. Grab a handful and make yourself at home
as you look through them for freelance opportunities.

You will be looking for two things: publications with articles that
are written by freelancers and thus are places where you could publish, too; and subjects that seem to fit the paper's mission but aren't
being covered. For example, if your daily newspaper rarely touches
on anything in the neighborhood where you live, maybe they could
use some freelance articles or a freelance correspondent, often called a
stringer. If nobody seems to be covering your city council or school
board, there's an opening for you. If the local churches or artists or
sports teams seem to be getting short shrift, maybe it's due to a lack of
manpower that you could help supply. Find the gap and fill it.

For dailies, the feature sections are your most likely freelance outlets. Usually they publish weekly or daily sections on food, home and
garden, travel, entertainment, arts and books, religion, and business.

There is generally something like "living" or "community" or "our town" with general features and columns. There may be a Sunday magazine or feature section. Big papers covering large metropolitan areas may have weekly sections focusing on particular neighborhoods. Look at the whole paper, but read these sections especially carefully.

Note the bylines and tags at the ends of stories. Are the writers identified as staff writers or are they listed as "special writers" or some other category that lets you know they're not part of the staff? Those are freelancers.

If you naturally gravitate to a particular section, that's your most likely place to find assignments. If you're like me, interested in just about everything, the whole paper is a possible market for your work. At small newspapers, one person edits everything, but at the larger papers, each section has its own editor. Look in the paper for the names of the editors. You can often find them on the editorial page. Sometimes newspapers run lists of editors in the front or local section, especially on slow news days, like Mondays. Or the editor may be identified in his byline, as in "Joe Smith, business editor."

Smaller papers may list the whole staff in the masthead, the box somewhere in the first few pages that provides basic information about the newspaper. If you see articles written by people who are not listed in the masthead, those articles were probably done by freelancers. Again, look for designations with the bylines or at the end of stories that tell you who the writers are.

The same method applies to specialty newspapers. Read the paper, study the masthead, and check out the bylines. Also look for blurbs asking for people to contribute articles. If you come up completely dry and the paper really interests you, you could telephone the newspaper. Ask if they use freelance work and whom you should address it to. The worst they can say is no.

I once called the *Catholic Sentinel* in Portland, Oregon, to ask if they used freelance. "Yes," said the editor, who answered the phone himself. "Do you pay?" I asked. "Oh, yes. We give you indulgences," he said with a chuckle. Indulgences in pre-Vatican II days meant you could get into Heaven sooner, spending less time purging your sins in Purgatory. After we laughed, the editor informed me that they do indeed pay in actual money, then gave me some ideas about how to get started.

You can also check the newspaper's website. The editors are usually listed, although you may have to scan the whole site to find the list. Look for "about us," "staff directory" or "contact us." Some newspaper sites offer guidelines for writers. Poke around until you find all the information that is there to be found. It can save a lot of running around and phone calls.

You can read a lot of newspapers online to see where you might fit in. David L. Ulin says that in the old days he was limited to the papers he could find at the newsstand, but now he has access to endless publications via the Internet. He urges freelancers to take advantage of this opportunity to study newspapers before pitching articles to them. After all, the biggest complaint of most editors is that writers who have never read their publication send material that is completely inappropriate. With the Internet, they have no excuse.

How Do You Get In?

I came into the newspaper business from the inside. I majored in journalism, interned at the *Milpitas Post* and went on to work at several newspapers in the San Francisco Bay Area. Over the years, I have covered every beat as a reporter and photographer. I have been a copy editor and editor of several community and special-interest newspapers, but I always wanted to freelance. I didn't like being a boss or having a boss, and I liked to control my own time and assignments.

Although pitching story ideas with a query letter, which we will discuss in Chapter 4, is standard procedure for magazines, it's only one of several paths into newspapers.

I became a regular contributor and eventually news editor of the *South Valley Times* after I answered a classified ad for freelance writers. When I called, the editor told me to find a story about the schools, write it up and turn it in. He didn't offer any money or promise that he would publish my story, just a chance to audition. I called the school district and told the superintendent I was looking for something to write about. As it happened, he wanted to promote his new computer system. That story got me in the door.

Contacts can lead to freelance work. I signed up for a job database with a now-defunct organization called Writer's Connection. They hooked me up with *Northern California Woman*, for which I wrote three articles, and with the *San Jose Mercury News* special sections editor, who gave me assignments for several years on topics such as wedding planning and home design.

A former professor with whom I kept in touch sent me a copy of the *Portuguese Heritage Journal*. This paper was not listed in *Writer's Market* and didn't have a website. I telephoned the editor in Florida and offered to cover Portuguese-American activities in the Bay Area. "Sounds good," he said. "How much do you charge?" I threw out a number. To my amazement, he said yes. I wrote many articles for him before the *Journal* went out of business.

Another freelance connection came from a friend who got a job editing a community newspaper in the San Jose area. She asked if I'd like to write stories for the *Los Gatos Weekly-Times* home and garden section. Soon I was writing almost one a week. A few months later, I was hired as a part-time staff writer for the *Saratoga News*, which was owned by the same company. When the editor left, I took her place.

My experience is not unusual with community newspapers. Dale Bryant of Silicon Valley Community Newspapers says she doesn't see many queries. More often, writers call or send letters saying they want to write for her company. She asks to see clips of their previous work, but even if they don't have any experience, her editors will give them an assignment to try. "What the editors are looking for really is a good working relationship with a very good writer," Bryant says. If the person wants a job and there aren't any openings, she will urge them to freelance for them first. That way the editor and the writer get to know each other, and it's easy to slip into place when a position becomes available.

In addition to sending out queries and keeping your eyes open for opportunities and contacts, it's important to let people know you're available. Join local writing organizations. Before either us went to work for the *Saratoga News* and its sister papers, Dale Bryant and I attended the same critique group. In fact, another friend took over my job as editor when I moved to Oregon. You can also meet writers and editors at conferences, such as the Northwest Journalism Conference, held every other year in Portland.

Establish an online presence by setting up a website. I was hired for a wonderful assignment about the Oregon Dunes National Recreation Area by the *Seattle Post-Intelligencer* after the editor found my website through a search for Oregon Coast writers. By posting information about yourself and providing links to published work, you can make your website your low-cost 24/7 publicist.

You have to be a bit of an entrepreneur, says Jennifer Meacham, a Vancouver, Washington, freelancer with credits in *The Oregonian, The Seattle Times, Vancouver Business Journal* and other papers. Founder of the Northwest Journalism Conference, she follows her own advice by maintaining a website with information about her work and links to her stories and by actively keeping in touch with the editors she wants to write for.

The first step in finding newspaper freelance opportunities is making yourself familiar with the market. Find the publications, then offer your services where you seem most likely to succeed. You may have to start at the bottom, but article by article, you can build a career as a freelance writer.

Exercise

• Collect as many newspapers as you can and read them, noting where they use freelance work. Then go to the library and analyze the newspapers there.

Study the market guides listed in the "Resources to Help You Find Markets for Your Writing" section at the back of this book. Do some browsing online to see which of the newspapers have websites and provide guidelines there for writers.

Develop a list of newspapers that use freelance work and look interesting to you. Include sections where your work might fit, along with what days they run, and the editors' names, postal addresses, phone numbers and e-mail addresses. You should have at least five possibilities on your list and may wind up with lots more.

Chapter 2

Developing Newspaper Article Ideas

Now that you have a list of possible markets for your work, what are you going to write about? In this chapter, we will look at where to get article ideas and how to shape them into stories that newspaper editors will buy.

Become an Idea Magnet

Article ideas are everywhere. You can find them in your work, your hobbies, the people you meet, or just driving down the street. They can come from the newspaper, the church bulletin, your club newsletter, a casual conversation with a friend, or a bumper sticker on the car in front of you on the freeway. All you have to do is open your mind to the possibilities.

Look around the room where you are sitting right now. How many story possibilities can you think of? I'll gaze at my office for a minute. I have sold several articles on computer problems. Anything computer-related could make a story. New equipment, virus protection, radiation coming from the monitor, carpal tunnel syndrome, and ways to design an effective website are all saleable subjects.

Maybe you're not technical. How about an article on what color you should paint your home office to inspire your best work? Or what kind of lighting is best? Is there a local decorator who specializes in home offices? Has anybody written a feature about him?

I have a full-spectrum light bulb to combat Seasonal Affective Disorder–SAD– which comes from a lack of natural sunlight. Newspapers run stories on SAD every winter. How do you know if you have it? What do the experts suggest to cope with this problem?

A spider plant sits on my window sill. What other kinds of plants grow well indoors, especially if you neglect them the way I do?

As I write, I'm drinking herb tea (Red Zinger), which raises a whole other area of article possibilities about the things people drink while they work. Which is better for you, coffee, tea, juice or bottled water? Is it possible to become addicted or make yourself sick with too much caffeine?

What else is in my office? Books, souvenirs, CDs, inspirational quotes, and much more. I'll bet there's an article idea lurking in every single item.

What's in the room where you write?

Look out the window. We recently received a rebate from the state of Oregon after we installed energy-saving double-paned windows. What other changes could a homeowner make to save energy and possibly earn a bonus from the government or the power company?

It's cold and damp here on the Oregon coast, so I can always write stories about ice, rain, snow, allergies to mold and mildew, wood stoves, studded tires, rust-proofing the car, storm-watching, or chimney sweeps. Where I used to live in California, it was hot and dry, and the focus was on air-conditioning and drought-tolerant gardening. Weather can also lead to articles on warm or cool clothing, which can lead to all kinds of related stories.

I live in the woods, but perhaps you live in the city or the suburbs or the desert. What you see out the window is bound to offer story ideas.

I keep a chart of local birds handy to identify the birds that come to the backyard feeder. When I lived in San Jose, I sold an article to

Bay Area Parent on setting up bird feeders as an activity for children. What kind of birds visit your back yard?

Don't limit yourself to ideas you can find at home. Get out into the community. Patricia MacAodha, who writes for community newspapers in her Portland, Oregon, neighborhood, is always looking for stories. "I really watch what's going on. You have to know your neighborhood. Walk around, read the posters, talk to people. Look at what the big papers are missing and give it the local touch."

Jennifer Meacham, who writes mostly business articles, says freelancers have an advantage over staff writers because they're not tied to their desks. They have more time to get involved in the community, which gives them more opportunities to hear what's going on.

What would interest the readers of the paper you want to write for? Wherever you go, whatever you do, keep them in mind. If, for example, you want to write for the *Erickson Tribune*, aimed at readers age 62 and older, think about what interests that age group. The editor's guidelines say, "Our readers are looking for ways to keep their minds and bodies in shape." How about some articles on education, health issues or exercise programs?

The *Erickson Tribune* also wants stories about relationships with adult children and grandchildren, how-to articles, and profiles of people over 62. I'll bet you can think of something that fits at least one of those criteria.

Before you decide you don't want to write about old folks, note that the *Erickson Tribune* pays $200 for an 800-word story and claims more than three *million* readers. The baby boomers becoming seniors constitute a huge market for newspapers aimed at their interests. Even if you're decades away from Social Security, it wouldn't hurt to brainstorm some ideas for baby boomer and senior publications. What do your parents talk about when you go to visit?

At the other end of the age spectrum, children can be a constant source of ideas. When my stepson was young, he inspired articles on color-blindness, fussy eating, left-handedness and the effects of being an only child. Hundreds of parenting publications offer information to parents of babies, toddlers, and older children. Even if you don't have children of your own, you surely know someone who does. What would they like to know?

One idea leads to another. Beginning writers worry about running out of ideas, but if you keep your mind open to the possibilities, that will never happen.

Things that you take for granted in your own life may be much more interesting to other people or to readers who live somewhere else. Think about what is interesting in your area. Where I live, it's the beach, the aquarium, the marine research center, the seafood, the weather, the lighthouses, and the dwindling logging industry. In another area, it might be the arts or technology or horses or casinos or ???? You can become an authority on your own area and write many, many articles.

Everything you have experienced in your life adds to the store of knowledge which can be applied to your writing. If you've rented, leased or bought a home or a car, you know about financing. If you have put work into that house or car, you know about home repairs, gardening, and car maintenance. If you're like most of us, you've had more than one type of job and know how to do many things. We all have families. We all experience births and deaths and learn the hard way about various health problems.

Try making a list with columns for education, work, hobbies, and family. Then start filling the columns with the things you know about. You will be surprised. In addition to whatever formal education you have had from kindergarten through high school or college, you have also learned other things. Think about religious studies, professional workshops, music lessons, participation in sports, even the cooking advice you learned from your mother, Girl Scouts, or a TV show. If you raise dogs, volunteer at a homeless shelter, have ten children, or work with the handicapped, you have stories. Once you start making that list, you will realize that you know about a lot of things. And if you don't know about something but you're curious, you can always learn.

If you find yourself running dry, here are a few other places to look for ideas:

- Newspaper and magazine articles. Yes, they already wrote that article, but you can use it as a springboard to a new idea or re-slant it for a new market.

• Eavesdropping. Come on, we all do it. If you hear a snatch of conversation that catches your interest, write it down and see how you can make it into a story.

• College course catalogs. They all offer the same basic English, math, science, and history classes, but you will also find other courses that are different, that are interesting, that might make a good article about a unique class or the professor teaching it.

• Classified ads in the newspaper. Especially look at the personals, the special notices, and the miscellaneous things for sale. Hmm, he's selling a complete Mariachi suit. What's the story behind that?

• Convention centers and big hotels: You could write an article about every group that comes in for a workshop or conference. Ask for a list of upcoming events.

• Calendars: Every season has its holidays and its stories. What's going on next month that could lead to an article? In addition to the obvious, every month is officially National Something month. Type "National Month" into your search engine, and you'll find plenty of wonderful and weird ideas. For example, October is not only Breast Cancer Awareness Month and Fire Prevention Month, but National Popcorn Poppin' Month and National Adopt-a-Dog Month. October 10 is National Angel Food Cake Day. Surely one of these will spark an idea.

Capture Those Ideas Before They Float Away

Ideas can come to you quickly, but they can also drift away in an instant. So always have paper and pen or pencil nearby to write them down. Keep writing supplies in your purse or pocket, by the bed, in the car, and wherever else you spend a lot of time. I get ideas in the shower, in the kitchen doing dishes, driving my car, walking the dog, even watching television shows. If I don't write them down, I usually discover that they're gone. If you can't put your idea on paper, come up with a memory aid, a set of initials or something else that will remind you. For example, if I want to write about snow tires, I program my brain to remember my idea the next time I drive the car.

The best ideas come from things that you yourself are interested in or know a lot about. Are you a quilter or a computer expert or a member of an organization working to help the homeless? Do you train guide dogs, climb mountains, or volunteer at a soup kitchen? Some writers dance from one topic to another. As your career moves along, you may want to specialize in a few subjects where you can continually build on your knowledge, develop files and sources and keep up with the latest developments, where you can in fact be considered an expert. This can lead to regular columns, something most of us want.

Ya Gotta Have an Angle

There are subjects and there are stories. What's the difference? An angle. You can't just say, "I want to write about llamas." What about llamas? If you say you want to write about llama obedience competitions, that's starting to look like a story. I watched such a competition at the Lincoln County Fair. It's similar to dog agility contests, except that unlike dogs, who zip through the tunnels and over the bridges in seconds, llamas stand there looking at their trainers. You can just tell they're thinking, "You want me to do what? I don't think so."

If you narrow the story down to a profile of a particular person who trains llamas for obedience competitions, or a feature about a competition coming up in your area, now you have a story.

Before you pitch a story, make sure you know what the angle is. Try giving your story a headline. It may not be the one that gets in the paper, but it makes very clear what your focus is going to be and it gives you and the editor something to call the story. Your pitch will also be stronger if you can name some of your sources. "Joe Smith up in Logsden has a herd of 20 llamas he has been training for seven years. As a member of the Happy Hopping Llamas, he can put me in touch with other owners. Plus, he's preparing for a competition next month. We can get pictures of the llamas in training." Who could resist such an article?

Perhaps you're aiming beyond the local weekly. Do you see a trend that has not been reported yet? Does it seem as if today's families are less likely to spend the holidays together? If you can pull together enough research, anecdotes and quotes to show a definite trend, an editor will be interested, especially if Christmas is coming.

Slanting Your Ideas for a Particular Newspaper

As mentioned in Chapter 1, every newspaper has a mission, whether it's to cover a particular geographic area, focus on a segment of society, or follow a particular industry. In order to sell your stories to a newspaper, you need to adapt them to fit that paper's mission. The most common need is for a "local angle." If you can tie your idea to someone or something in the community that the paper covers, you're much more likely to get it published. Tell the editor why her readers will be interested. If you can't do that, try another newspaper or another story.

Finding the connection can be easy or difficult, depending on the subject. If you want to write a feature about a local author, no problem. If you want to write about antique glass, find a dealer who sells it, an expert who collects it, or suggest places to buy it in your area.

If you want to write about air pollution, you'll need to stretch a little farther and find someone in the community who is doing research or fighting for new legislation or maybe someone who is polluting like crazy and doesn't care. Maybe there is a business that does things in a new way to avoid air pollution. Is there someone who makes or drives electric cars in your area? Is solar power out of vogue or is a contractor in your town doing something new and wonderful with it?

Each year around September 11, newspapers will run stories about the terrorist attacks and what has happened since then. Many local angles can be found: people who were in New York or Washington, D.C., when it happened, people who lost loved ones, people who are working on charity projects for the bereaved, people who have been inspired to become police officers or firefighters since 9/11, security changes at the local airport, the vulnerability of tall buildings in your area, young men and women who were subsequently sent to fight in the Middle East.

In the same way, you can look back at Hurricane Katrina. What has happened since the levee broke in New Orleans? Have people found new homes? Have some of them moved to your town? Is there a levee in your area that might give way?

Natural and man-made disasters can strike anywhere. What event changed everything in your town?

You can write stories related to the economy. What are rising gas prices doing to tourism? In Western Oregon, you might write about lumber mills closing down and fishermen looking for other ways to make a living. We have seen a rise in unemployment, which means an increase in people who are homeless or struggling to survive. I have seen people sleeping in the doorway at my church and begging for money in the parking lot at the Fred Meyer store. Writing about such people puts a human face on an abstract problem. Are people doing anything to help, or are they ignoring the situation? Either way, you can find a story in it.

Perhaps the daily or weekly newspaper would run a feature on the food bank and how people can contribute. You might slant the same idea for a senior publication by profiling the many volunteers over 70 who work at the food bank. Or maybe the local Baptist church has designated the food bank as its special charity. Perhaps *Baptists Today* would be interested. You could take the story in a different direction for the *Business Journal* by looking at efforts to bring in new industries that will provide high-paying jobs.

Every school district has both problems and accomplishments to write about. Colleges and universities yield countless stories about classes, research discoveries, arts activities, publications, cultural events, and new programs. As a freelance writer, you can ask to be put on the university public relations department's mailing list. They will send you press releases about everything that's going on.

If you have an idea but no market, ask yourself who would be interested in this subject. Then find the paper that those people read. Your ideas need to be interesting not only to you but to the market for which you are aiming. As Jill Dick, author of a British book called *Freelance Writing for Newspapers*, says, "A fisherman baits his hook not with what he likes, but with what fish like." Think about what readers want to read and aim your stories accordingly.

Ads, Media Releases and Articles

Writers who are not trained in journalism may not be aware of the differences between advertisements, media releases and articles.

Advertisements

Ads, as you know, are paid for by the advertiser. In all but the smallest papers, they are produced by a completely different department from the editorial department that produces the articles for the paper. By nature, ads are one-sided and designed to convince readers to buy something. It is interesting to note that advertising, not subscriptions, is what pays the bills for most newspapers.

Roundups, articles that are basically a list of products or companies, are sometimes tied to advertising. I have even worked for publications that will only list a particular business in a roundup if that business buys an ad. At papers with more ethical policies, the editors will simply pass the word to the advertising salespeople, who in turn suggest to their clients that now would be a good time to advertise in connection with the feature to be run.

When I studied journalism, my professors painted a picture of an impermeable wall between editorial and advertising, but in the twenty-first century, it's more like a chain link fence with big holes between the links. In fact, there is a genre of journalism called "advertorial," in which advertisers sponsor articles or whole sections. These can actually be lucrative sources of income for freelancers. Some of the stories I have written on weddings and home decorating appeared in "special advertising sections." If you don't mind a little shameless commerce, don't overlook these sections as possible freelance opportunities. Just be clear what you are writing.

If your piece is not an advertorial, then include whoever or whatever ought to be in the story, regardless of whether they ever have or will purchase an ad.

The ad sales department may pressure you to write something favorable about a company which buys advertising or its product. Walk the line between touting a newspaper's customers and reporting carefully; the readers need to be able to trust that you are writing a balanced, unbiased story.

Media Releases

Media releases are written to publicize events, new products, achievements, and other things for which someone wants publicity. Corporations, politicians, nonprofit organizations, universities, and government agencies employ writers to produce media releases. Editors receive piles of media releases every day.

Many of these public relations pieces are well-written and sound just like regular articles, but the editors and savvy readers know that they were written for the purpose of getting free publicity. They are designed to make the subject look good and rarely give more than one side of a story.

Writing press releases pays well and is another avenue where freelance writers can make money. Your paycheck will, however, come from the organization, not from the newspaper. You may find it difficult to sell freelance articles that have any connection to your public relations work, with some editors classifying you as a PR flak and assuming that anything you submit is simply publicity for your client.

A staff reporter or freelance writer may use a media release as a starting point for his own story, but should go beyond the information in the press release, doing additional interviews and research to present a complete and original story.

Has It Been Done Before?

You might have a great idea, but if the newspaper in question just did a piece on the subject you are suggesting, it's not likely to buy another one soon. If it did something a year or more ago, read the earlier article and try pitching a fresh approach. If several competing publications have published articles about a particular subject recently, you may have a hard time selling a story on the same subject. By the way, telling an editor that her competitors ran a story on the subject will *not* make her want to run a story on the same thing.

How do you find out what has been done before? In the days before computers, this was a lot more difficult. It required looking at actual newspapers, either at the library or at the newspaper office itself. In school, people of my generation learned to use the *Reader's Guide to Periodical Literature*, which was a collection of books one would find in the reference section of the library. You would look up your topic, see what articles had been published, write down the titles and dates on a slip of paper, give it to the librarian and wait while she disappeared into the archives, coming back an hour later with a yellowed newspaper. Later came microfilm, which also required a trip to the library and a look through the *Reader's Guide*.

Of course many smaller periodicals were not indexed in the guides so freelancers needed to go through stacks of newspapers to see if an idea had been covered recently.

If you were lucky, you could visit the newspaper's "morgue," the library where past articles were kept, and search for what ran before. However, at many small newspapers, the morgue consisted—and still does—of copies of the newspaper bound together in massive books which you look through one page at a time, an interesting but time-consuming task.

Then came computers, hallelujah. Although you might still have to read older, pre-Internet stories at the library or by paging through back issues at the newspaper office, some papers publish their articles online now. Not only can you read the current issue, but you can search the archives for articles that ran before. Some papers charge a small fee to let you into their online database. If you are going to look there fairly often, it's worth it to pay the price. If it's a one-shot deal, there are other ways around it. Check the resource section at the back of this book for databases that publish newspaper articles online. Variations of the old *Reader's Guide* still exist online, along with other electronic databases that list published articles, but if you're aiming for a particular newspaper, go there first.

You can also enter your topic in your favorite search engine and find articles that way. Today Google.com is one of the most popular search engines, but don't overlook other sites, such as Yahoo.com, or Ask.com.

The best topics may have only a few listings, which means they're worth writing about but haven't been overdone. Save the articles you find to help you with your own story. If you can't find any listings, either you're not using the right search terms or your topic is so obscure that editors haven't shown any interest in it. Perhaps the subject is simply too local to be included online, but it still might be a good thing for you to write.

If the situation warrants, ask people involved in your subject if they know of anything that has been published recently. They may have files of their own which they will copy for you or they can e-mail links to useful websites.

Come up with Something Different

Editors look to freelancers for the stories they can't get. Perhaps they don't have enough staff to cover a particular neighborhood or subject, or they can't afford to devote the time a complicated story would take. Or maybe, through your own activities and contacts, you have access to ideas that they haven't thought of.

"The writers who take the time and have the dedication to research topics that are being ignored by the mainstream media get our attention and get our dollars," says Ted Taylor, editor of the *Eugene (Oregon) Weekly*.

If you approach an editor with an intriguing idea that fits his paper's mission, he will give you a chance. Sally Abrahms, who has been published in the *New York Times, Boston Globe, Hartford Courant,* and other major dailies, had not written a single newspaper article when she pitched a story on parental kidnapping to the *New York Daily News.* But they bought it, and that led to a long series of articles on family legal issues. "I was not an established writer. I had no credentials, but I had a good idea."

If you can come up with a new angle—a trend, a larger story that is yours, you're in.

Pictures?

Let's talk about photographs. This may seem off the subject, but it really isn't. When an editor is putting a page together, he or she looks for "art," the newspaper term for photos, drawings, maps, charts or any other non-text entity that can dress up the page. A story without art is a big gray block of type. Without art, your story may wind up below or next to another story that might not be as interesting but has good pictures. Editors appreciate writers who consider the art along with the story. If you are an artist or a good photographer and can provide your own art, you have a huge advantage when writing for small and medium-sized publications. Not only will editors be more inclined to buy your stories, but you will get paid extra for every photo or drawing.

Many small-circulation papers expect staff reporters to take their own pictures. The editors hope that freelancers will do the same. Again, technology is on your side. In the old days, cameras were big and complicated. You had to know about light meters and f-stops and carry a whole bag of lenses for different shots. You might even have been expected to process your film in your own darkroom. But today's cameras are small enough to carry in a purse or backpack and so automated that most people can take publishable photos.

In the recent past, newspapers wanted slides, color prints, or black and white prints. Not anymore. Of the newspapers surveyed for this book, only one was still using film. Editors not only expect writers to submit their stories over the Internet, but they want their pictures the same way. If you haven't yet switched to a digital camera, invest the money.

If you really don't want to or can't take pictures, you can still help provide photographs. One of the easiest ways is to team up with a photographer and share the bylines and the pay. Some husband-and-wife teams do this regularly.

Another possibility is to use others' photographs. The Library of Congress, Prints and Photographs Division, and the National Archives, Still Picture Branch, both offer photos. Each government division, including the U.S. Fish and Wildlife Service, NASA, and the Department of Defense, also have pictures you can obtain for a nominal reproduction fee.

Many state and local government agencies, historical associations, libraries, museums, zoos, chambers of commerce, tourist bureaus, and other publicly funded organizations will provide photographs on request. Companies whose products you are writing about will be glad to give you pictures.

In addition, all kinds of associations and societies have photos to offer. For example, when I wrote about mushrooms for *Oregon Coast*, the local mushroom society had wonderful photos that were far better than mine and really dressed up the article.

The people you interview may also have photos to lend you. They may in fact prefer you use their pictures.

Finally, there are photo agencies–Shutterstock.com is one–that make their living selling pictures. A web search for your subject plus the word *photos* will yield more pictures than you could ever use. You can even buy photographs on eBay.

Copyright Applies to Photos, Too

It is possible to copy digital images from almost anywhere on the Internet and save them on your hard drive. As a practical matter, most of these photos are too low resolution to provide a clear image when printed on paper. If you do download them, make sure you never pass them off as your own. Copyright laws apply to pictures as well as words. Contact the copyright owner and ask for permission before you use anyone else's photos.

Be conscientious about giving credit to the photographer. Let the editor know where you got the picture and who should get the photo credit. The young man who loaned me those mushroom pictures for *Oregon Coast* not only got credit, he got paid for them. He didn't expect it, but he deserved it.

Larger newspapers usually have their own photographers and use them exclusively. However, be prepared to help the editor with ideas for pictures. She may ask you to provide names and contact information to set up photo shoots of people you include in your article.

Is It Doable?

As you're brainstorming ideas, consider how you would approach each and choose the ones that seem most workable. If you come up with a blockbuster of an idea, then discover that you have no idea how to do it or don't have the resources to do it, you might have to let the story go.

As you consider story ideas, think about where you will find the information you need. Do you know a lot about it already? Are written materials available? Is there an expert at hand? Is what you need easy to obtain or will it take you months of research to learn enough to write an article which could turn out to pay $50?

Perhaps you can do one piece of a topic now and learn enough to do a broader story for another publication later. Be conscious of how much time it will take and how much time you have.

Know your other limitations, too. Are you willing to talk to people who would rather not be interviewed, get wet and dirty, or enter a war zone? If you are unusually shy, physically handicapped, tied down by children, or can't get away from your day job, look for stories that don't require you to travel or conduct interviews in person.

Don't pitch a story you can't do. The world is full of article ideas. All you have to do is reach out and grab one and tailor it to the needs of the newspaper you want to write for.

Exercise

• Using the list of newspapers you compiled during your market research, try to come up with at least three article ideas.

In one or two paragraphs per idea, list a possible headline, topics to be included, sources of information and art that might go with it.

• List the places where you think this article might be published.

• Take each idea and write down several different ways you might approach it for different newspapers or different sections of the same newspaper. Have fun with this. Sometimes what seems at first like a crazy idea turns out to be the best one.

Chapter 3

Types of Newspaper Articles

Freelance articles can end up on any page of any newspaper, but certain sections are more open to freelance than others. In this chapter, we will look at some of the most popular freelance options in detail, then describe some other types of articles that you might also be able to sell. As you read these, remember that you can develop almost any topic into any one of these article types–or all of them. Remember the llama rancher? You could write a profile on him, put together a story on how to get started in the llama business, write a travel piece on where to see llamas, write about your personal experience trying to train a llama, or even do an opinion piece about how llamas should or should not be allowed in your neighborhood. There are plenty of books on llamas. How about a book review?

You may find that a particular kind of article appeals to you more than the others. Look for published examples to see what newspapers publish and to see how the writers present them. How long are these articles? How many sources do they quote? Are they written in the first person, using *I*, second person, addressing the reader as *you*, or third person, using *he* or *she*? Ask yourself what caused the editor to choose this article for his newspaper? Then look at how you can apply the answers to your own article ideas.

Personality Profiles

Profiles, word portraits of interesting people, are one of the easiest things to write and to sell. Nearly every publication uses profiles, and you can often write them with just a little bit of research and one interview. William L. Rivers, a renowned journalism professor from Stanford University and author of *Free-lancer and Staff Writer*, writes that "nearly half the articles now appearing in popular magazines are woven around interesting characters, their hopes, their problems, foibles and adversities and how they finally got around or over the hurdles in their paths." Ditto for newspapers, except that your profiles will probably be shorter and use fewer sources.

Celebrities get a lot of press, but ordinary people can also be fascinating. And they're much more accessible. You run into them in everyday life, read about them in the local paper or hear about them from other people. Possibilities: your church pastor, the guy who teaches karate at the gym, the woman who has a big sign in front of her house that says, "Quilts for sale." What about the person who owns the adult video store where Christian groups picket every weekend? Who is he? Why does he stay open? How does he feel about the picketers?

Writers, sculptors, musicians, actors and others in the arts are all natural profile subjects, as are collectors, landscapers, storytellers, veterans, immigrants, and centenarians. You could write about the woman who delivers your mail and always has a treat for the dog, the guy who goes mushroom hunting every fall, or the grandma who makes the best clam chowder in town. Perhaps you know someone famous who might not talk to big-name journalists, but would be willing to talk to you.

Everyone has a story. Sometimes you may need to push a little to get them to tell it, but they have a story. Find out enough of that story to interest an editor, and you'll get an assignment.

For a well-rounded profile, you need to collect as much information as you can about the person. Not only will you report what she says, but describe how she looks and acts. Provide some background on her life and share what others have to say about her.

In writing the profile, as with all your other writing, grab the reader's attention right away. Put us in a scene with the person, showing her doing or saying something unusual or intriguing. Give us a curious fact, an anecdote, or even a joke, whatever it takes to get the reader to read on.

In fiction, we often talk about the need to "show, don't tell." The same applies to newspaper features. Paint the picture with specific details. What is he wearing? Does his baseball cap cover a bald head? Do her hands glitter with rings on every finger? Are there books piled on every table? Does a dog greet you at the door—or a parrot? What kind of music is playing? What does the house smell like? What art or photographs decorate the walls? Does he offer you strong coffee, herb tea or a glass of homemade wine? Did she bake you a cake? Don't just give us the facts; make us feel as if we are there with you talking to that person.

As with other story types, a profile needs an angle. We don't need to know everything this person has ever done, just the experiences that will interest the readers of this particular publication. Go back to the llama trainer; does it really matter that he was the state spelling bee champion all four years of high school? It isn't likely you'd include this bit of information in your profile of him unless your article was going to run in a periodical aimed at high school students. For most articles and for most papers you would want to focus on how he came to be a llama trainer and how he does his work.

Whether your subject is a llama trainer or the mayor of Minneapolis, the reader wants to connect with him as a human being. Use direct quotes to let us hear how he talks. Give us a taste of his accent and attitude. How does he react when you ask him a difficult question? Does he stiffen up or lean back and smile? Does he offer to take you on a tour? Does he speak freely or does he insist on having his press agent nearby to monitor every word that goes into your notebook?

General-interest newspapers run lots of profiles. You can also sell personality profiles to specialty newspapers. Remember, every group has one—hobbyists, members of each religion, military families, bluegrass music lovers, doll collectors, fraternal organizations—everybody's got a paper, even if you don't see them on the newsstand. Your job is to figure out which paper would be interested in this person. You may be able to write about the same person for several different papers, focusing on different aspects of his life. Maybe that llama rancher is still involved in spelling bees, but now he travels the state judging contests. Perhaps he's also a deacon in his church. Ask, "What do you do in your spare time?" or "Is there anything about you that people would be surprised to know?" (And that editors would like to share with their readers?) If you see a clue—a plaque on the wall, a souvenir, or anything else that makes you wonder, ask.

Refrigerator Journalism

In the newspaper world, some of the best sellers are what is sometimes called refrigerator journalism. These are the articles people clip out of the paper and stick to the fridge with a magnet or save in a file folder. They keep them because they're useful. I have some of those sitting in a box on my desk right now. One tells how to get mildew off aluminum window frames. Another is about the new trails at Cape Perpetua National Park. And another is a feature about a museum that I plan to visit.

Many newspapers run columns labeled "News You Can Use." I thought I made it up when I offered the idea of "News You Can Use" to the newspaper where I did my internship. My editor groaned, but she approved it. The weekly column contained useful tidbits, such as events to attend, telephone hotlines for various problems, auditions for upcoming plays, lists of art exhibits, places to cut down Christmas trees, and meetings of area organizations.

Many garden sections run lists of tasks to do each month, such as pruning rose bushes or planting bulbs. Other clippable garden features might include a list of nature-friendly weed-killers or ways to get rid of slugs. Perfect for the fridge.

Recipes are another good example of useful news. How about a list of the different kinds of apples and what each is best used for? Or a collection of ingredients one can combine to make smoothies?

Refrigerator stories have to be useful, something somebody wants to save. I clipped the Cape Perpetua story because it sounds like a wonderful day trip for my husband and me to take on the next sunny day we have off. I clipped the mildew story because here on the coast, we've got it, and it's hard to get rid of.

Travel articles are great candidates for the refrigerator, especially the articles that tell how to get there, where to stay, where to eat, what to see, and where to find more information.

I have often clipped articles about new restaurants I want to try, stores that sell something I need, or items about upcoming exercise classes that I might take. Freebies attract people: free rabies shots, free hearing tests, free used books. Maybe you should write an article on where to get free things in your town.

Most refrigerators are not big enough to hold a whole newspaper page. People are more likely to save articles that are short and easy to read. Lists, question-and-answer features, and sidebars—information boxes that run beside a larger story—may not win you a Pulitzer prize, but they might win a place on the fridge between the children's art and the grocery list.

What follows are two of the most popular forms for refrigerator journalism.

Roundups

Look at the cover of any women's magazine. You see lists: ten ways to please your man, eight thigh-trimming exercises, tips for stress-free holiday shopping. They're called roundups, and newspapers use them, too. A business publication may look at the top MBA programs. At Christmas, you're likely to see roundups covering the best new toys on the market, tips for decorating your home, and easy homemade gifts. The travel section might list ten ways to make traveling with children less stressful.

The sole mission of a roundup story is to convey information. Certainly this is not the type of article you dream about writing, but editors love them and readers use them. In fact, sometimes you might volunteer to do a roundup piece because you want to research this topic for yourself. You're looking for things for the kids to do during the summer? Why not research the possibilities and make a few dollars at the same time?

I have written roundup pieces on everything from where to get a good hamburger to a survey of services offered by local funeral par lors. Travel sections may run "best cruises" or "best dog parks." The food section might do a roundup of local wineries, culinary schools, or places to eat pancakes. In the spring, newspapers look at wedding-related topics, such as the most romantic places to get married or the best places to hold a reception.

A roundup piece consists of a few introductory paragraphs and then a list. For each item, you give pertinent information, such as address, phone number, website, and a brief description. Most of your time will be spent gathering information and deciding which items should be included. The writing will fall into a framework and should be relatively easy.

How-To Articles

How-to's help the reader solve a problem. The headlines will offer how to lose weight, make prize-winning fudge, prepare your home for an earthquake, save money for retirement, find a dog trainer, etc.

Specialized publications print specialized how-to's. Craft newspapers might tell how to make a gingerbread house, put together a quilt or make a needlepoint picture. Antiques publications tell how to distinguish valuable jewelry from cheap, how to organize a shot-glass collection, or where to find Victorian furniture. A parenting paper will tell how to choose a preschool, how to deal with a child who refuses to eat vegetables, or how to blend your children and stepchildren into a happy family.

In a general-interest newspaper, the various special sections, such as travel, gardening, or cooking, are the most likely markets for how-to articles.

A recipe is a perfect example of a how-to. It tells you what you need and how to put it together. A recipe for Hot Texas Chili is just as much a how-to as an article on how to install a solar water heater.

You don't need to be an expert on the subject you are writing about. You just need to do a little research or interview someone who is. Even if you are an expert, quotes from other sources will give your story more credibility. If you are writing for a paper with national or widespread regional circulation, including sources from different parts of the country will help to sell your story.

In a how-to, clarity overrules creativity. However, writing that is enjoyable to read is still important.

A how-to needs to be about something the reader of the publication which runs it wants to know. An article about how to fix a broken portable CD player probably wouldn't sell because most people would simply buy a new one. But they would read about how to buy that new CD player or how to create a stock portfolio or how to improve one's relationships.

Most of us don't care how to pack a parachute because we'll never use one, but if you're writing for beginning skydivers, they really might want to read such an article. The rest of us would be more interested in how to pack an airplane carry-on bag so that it's not too heavy and doesn't get us in trouble at the security checkpoint.

The topic needs to be meaty enough to give you something worth writing but focused enough to fit within the allotted space, usually no more than 1,000 words. That means you won't be able to cover everything about preparing for a trip or even how to pack all of one's luggage, but you should be able to do a clear, complete piece about packing that carry-on.

With how-to articles, unlike most other types of articles, you will probably write in the second person, addressing the reader as "you" (as I am in this book). Picture yourself having a conversation in which you share this information with your reader. "First you preheat the oven and grease the pan. Then you…"

As always, grab their interest with an intriguing opening paragraph. You might start by telling how this article will make their lives better. Or you could set the scene by telling the story of one person who successfully used these techniques: "Stella had decided she would never be a size 12 again, but by making a few small adjustments to her diet, she lost 50 pounds and wowed her classmates at her 20-year high school reunion." Another way to begin is to use interesting statistics: "Over the last year, 20 percent of airline passengers were stopped at the security gate for carrying items that were not allowed on board. Some missed their flights. Don't be one of them."

Next, spell out the process step by step, as clearly as possible. Your language can be casual, even funny, but keep the focus on clear instructions. "Boil 8 minutes or until the pasta is flexible but not too soft." "Plant pointed side down six inches deep." If you use terms that might be unfamiliar, explain them. Include warnings where needed, e.g., "Wear gloves and don't let the solution touch your skin."

If possible, ask someone to read your article and try the steps to make sure you didn't leave anything out. Readers get upset when they use a recipe and discover you forgot to mention the cup of sugar—or told them to add a cup when you meant a tablespoon. And, of course, when the editor discovers he ran your mistake…well, just don't expect any calls with offers of future assignments.

If possible, include photographs or suggest illustrations the periodical can run with your how-to. Illustrations make it easier for the reader to follow your instructions, and they dress up the page.

Finish by summing up what the reader will have accomplished and giving him a good reason to take action. "If you start this diet right now, you'll be ready for swimsuit season with a trim new figure." "If you plant your daffodil bulbs this weekend, they'll poke their pretty yellow heads up out of the dirt in late February, letting you know that spring is on its way."

Op-Eds

If how-to articles or roundups leave you aching to express yourself more freely, op-ed pieces and reviews offer wonderful relief. In most sections of the newspaper, writers are supposed to keep their opinions to themselves and provide an unbiased look at whatever the topic is. Not here.

Editorials are opinion pieces written by newspaper editors and staff writers. Usually unsigned, they represent the official view of the paper. On the page *opposite* the *editorial* page is the op-ed page. (Get it? *Op-ed?*) There you will find more opinion pieces, but these are written by syndicated columnists, local VIPs, and *freelance writers.* Look at the bylines and the tags at the ends of the articles to see who these writers are and gauge your chances of joining their ranks.

The daily newspaper is one of the best sources for op-ed ideas. If a subject is getting a lot of press lately, the editor of a daily newspaper will be looking for op-ed pieces on that subject. But look also at the situations you encounter in your daily life. This is a chance to point out problems that should be getting some attention but haven't yet. Is the traffic on your commute getting so bad you can't go another day without doing something about it? Have you just discovered that your son's school no longer teaches kids the multiplication tables? Are you overwhelmed by the cost of groceries or appalled by the prices of prescription drugs?

Like the major daily newspapers, most smaller newspapers run opinion pieces. Look into the alternative weeklies, small-town papers, and the free papers that are distributed to residents in your area. These are usually easier to crack than the big dailies. However, everything local papers publish has to have a local angle. If can find a local connection, your piece qualifies.

For special-interest publications, consider the reader and speak to his interests. An op-ed piece on changes to social security would likely find a more willing editor at a senior newspaper than a paper targeted to a readership of young parents.

Op-ed pieces are written in the first person. They include the author's opinion, backed up with evidence from life experience as well as research. They usually have a connection to current events and may be written in response to previous editorials or letters to the editor. The best ones connect the personal to the universal. In other words, by telling the story of what happened to one person or group of people, they make a point that we can all relate to.

Dale Bryant, executive editor for Silicon Valley Community Newspapers, notes that her readers are anxious to read about issues. They are much more interested in the economy, transportation, or the latest scandal at City Hall than they are in how it felt to watch your son hit his first home run. "That's not going to fly in Silicon Valley," Bryant says—unless you can find a way to relate your personal story to a bigger, more universal story. If youth baseball programs are dwindling due to city cutbacks, suddenly Johnny's home run becomes relevant.

The *Christian Science Monitor*'s guidelines state it well: "We aim to provide fodder for the public conversation that's both engaging and enlightening. If it's a subject people care about, and it's well-written, we'd probably be interested in seeing it."

Most opinion pieces range from 500 to 750 words. Some are as short as 300 words, while others are 1,000 words or longer. Check the guidelines for specific newspapers to see their requirements. Don't bother sending in a piece that is substantially longer or shorter than specified.

Overall, a good opinion piece should contain the following:

- A catchy title. The editor may not use it, but it gives you and the editor something to call it and provides a focus for the piece.
- A strong opening that grabs the readers.
- A clear thesis—a point. What are you trying to say?
- An original slant on the subject, something that is different from what has already been said.
- Timeliness. Why are you bringing this up now? Can you connect it to a recent event, a holiday, an anniversary, a report that just came out, or something else people are talking about? If it is linked to a news event, don't wait more than a day or two to write it and send it. News grows stale quickly.
- Logic. Pour out your emotions in your first draft. Don't worry about anything except getting them down on paper. But then go back and make sure your views are expressed clearly, with information to back them up. Take out any unnecessary name-calling, obscenities, browbeating or ridiculing of folks who may disagree with you. It is more effective to be persuasive rather than antagonistic.
- Facts and examples. Bring in your research, experiences from real life and any other evidence you need to reinforce your case. Tell about real people and how your issue has affected them.
- Solutions. Offer a fix to the problem. Don't just rant; tell us what you want us to do.
- A focused conclusion. Boil your conclusion down to one strong statement that sums up your point. Don't leave the reader any doubt about what you want to say.

Remember, these are not your English 1A essays. You can allow your personality to show. You can use creative metaphors, paint scenes, adopt a style all your own. You can be serious or sarcastic, heartfelt or tongue-in-cheek. Think about Andy Rooney and his grumpy old man routine or Jerry Seinfeld asking, "What's the deal with...?"

Think about the subjects in which you are an expert because of work, education or life experiences. If you are a teacher, you know about the schools and the problems they face. If you have children, you know the challenges of parenting today. If you are a veteran, you may have personal experience in combat. If you have been a victim of domestic violence, you know more about that subject than you ever wanted to know. Travel, hobbies, home maintenance, health problems, legal troubles, buying a home, driving a car—just about everything you do could lead to an opinion piece.

Consider the holidays. What about a commentary on patriotism—or the Patriot Act—for the Fourth of July? Look also at anniversaries—D-Day, Roe v. Wade, Watergate, Columbine, 9/11, Hurricane Katrina. Any major local, national or international event can lead to an editorial comparing the situation then and now. Did you live through an experience in your childhood that colors the way you look at things happening now? Write about it.

When in doubt, ponder what stirs your emotions. "The best starting point is your point of maximum indignation," according to Harvard journalism professor John Lenger. What is *your* point of maximum indignation?

Reviews

Although we tend to think of books when we hear the word "review," reviews are written and published every day about many other things, including CDs, DVDs, plays, operas, dance performances, computer software, cameras, cars, cruises, restaurants, hotels, even the latest hybrid roses offered in the seed catalog. That means lots of opportunities for you as a writer.

Like op-eds, these are opinion pieces, but they center on a specific product or experience. A review is more than just thumbs up or thumbs down, four stars or no stars. It is a blend of description and evaluation. Not only do we introduce readers to the subject of our review, but we test the waters for them and give them our informed opinion.

Reviews can be a good way to get some valuable publishing credits and a little cash for having your say. Reviews don't necessarily pay as much as feature articles. Most earn in the $50 to $150 range, but they require less research, take less time to write—some are as short as 200 words—and you can often double or triple your money by reselling the same review to several publications that have different readerships.

Reviews can lead to other work for publications you've been wanting to get into. Sally Abrahms wrote reviews on books about family legal issues to get her first clips from the *Los Angeles Times*, *New York Times*, *Philadelphia Inquirer* and other major newspapers. Being able to say she had written for those papers opened the doors for bigger assignments at major metropolitan dailies.

Think beyond the obvious. For example, readers of recreational vehicle and boating publications might be interested in reviews of single-dish cookbooks or products designed for cooking in small spaces. Someone planning to buy a digital camera will read reviews of what's on the market. Whatever the specialty is, a newspaper or website will probably carry reviews of things their readers might want to buy or do. Why not write them?

Most editors will not publish a review that arrives in the mail from an unknown writer. They prefer to assign reviews to writers who have proven abilities. To get on an editor's list of writers, you might need to write some sample reviews.

This should not be a heavy burden if you review something you already enjoy. You can review the last book you read or the next one you pick off the shelf. You can review the concert you're scheduled to attend this weekend. You can write about the CD you just bought. You could hit the jackpot and not only get an assignment for a future review but sell the ones you have already written.

You can get experience writing reviews for online websites such as www.amazon.com, www.Barnesandnoble.com, and www.bookreporter .com, along with other venues, such as club or church newsletters and websites for organizations to which you belong. They may not pay money, but your reviews will be published with your byline. If you have your own website, there's no reason you can't publish reviews there, too. Anything that gives you a sample to send out is worth trying.

When you have several sample reviews, write a brief cover letter and send them to the editor of your choice. Suggest a review you would like to write for their publication. Do not expect to start with assignments to review books by best-selling authors or popular movies. Offer to write about something that is new, fresh, or local. Suggest reviewing a hometown production, not a famous performing artist on tour. The staff writers are already fighting over those assignments.

Writing an effective review is an art. In an average of two manuscript pages, you have to pack a lot of information. The same elements apply to all types of reviews: Hook the reader; give the basics of what it is and where people can buy it, see it, or experience it; provide some background, and tell us what you think. The review should contain:

- A theme or idea that ties the review's concepts together
- Basic information (such as title, author, publisher, and price for a book review)
- Background on this item or similar ones
- Your evaluation, in particular how well the item achieves its intended purpose, with some examples to back up your opinion

It is also important to meet the requirements of whatever publication you're writing for. This includes length, format, and content. Some editors want more description and less opinion. Some reviews are very straightforward, while others are humorous or academic or written for the interests of a specific audience. If you were writing a book review for a young adult periodical, for example, you would definitely slant it toward the interests of teens.

Information is the key to a review. You could say "I didn't like it" or "I liked it" in one sentence. But that's not enough. We need to know why. A review is a description by a consumer who is more informed than the average person and shares that information with the rest of the world.

David L. Ulin of the *L.A. Times,* speaking of book reviews, warns against writing reviews that are so negative they're just cruel. "They shouldn't be like a mugging. But at the same time, I think if a book is really problematic to a reviewer, the reviewer needs to say that, and in terms as unmuddied as possible. I think that kind of review is necessary to the critical dialogue. It's not just patting people on the head. Otherwise, we're just shills for the book business."

In general, a review is not just "criticism" in the sense of "good" or "bad." It's a chance for you to analyze and make a judgment based on what you have seen and what you know, to share with the world what you have discovered.

Pick out the most outstanding aspect of whatever you're reviewing and use that as the lynchpin that holds your review together. Keep your writing lively, using active verbs and specific language.

Remember that this is not a school book report. If it is not interesting and well-written, editors won't buy it and readers won't read it. But if grabs the reader's interest and gives this person the information he needs, editors will buy it, readers will read it.

If you don't see reviews of the thing you're interested in, contact the editor and see if she's interested. Have some sample reviews ready. She might say yes.

Travel Articles

Look at the travel section of your daily newspaper. Not only are there pieces on various destinations, but advice on how to pack, how to make reservations, how to plan a trip, how to keep the kids amused in the car, and more. Among the guides to particular cities or special attractions, you can find offbeat personal experience accounts of anything from getting lost at the airport to learning to eat escargot. As long as an idea involves travel, you might be able to hang a story on it. And you could adapt it for seniors, parents, book-lovers, the disabled, executives, and many other groups with their own newspapers.

I recently read a terrific travel-section story in which the writer never left the airport. It took place at "Gate 66." After a pilot called in sick, it was announced that the San Francisco to Boston flight would be at least three hours late, probably longer. While most people grumbled, one man got out his guitar and started playing. Another man pulled a harmonica out of his pocket and joined in. Pretty soon it turned into a party, with people calling out requests and singing along. The article was a refreshing piece that showed human beings abandoning their schedules and turning off their cell phones to relate to each other—except for one cranky New Yorker who added a comic note to the story.

For many travel articles, the writer visits a destination then writes about it, offering information so readers can follow in his footsteps. If the place has been written about over and over, you will need to come up with a fresh angle to interest editors and readers.

Under the umbrella of travel, you can write many types of articles:

- **Profile/interview.** Write about people you meet on your journey, people who work at the places you visit, or interesting fellow travelers. Another kind of profile can look at a business and how it compares to similar businesses where your readers live.

- **How-to.** How to pack, how to get good deals on travel reservations, how to stay healthy on the road, how to stay on your diet, how to take good pictures, how to keep your kids amused, how to avoid getting blisters on your feet, etc.

- **Personal experience.** This is not just the self-involved writing you put in your diary. Tell us a real story that can amuse and inform the reader at the same time. If you can make it humorous, all the better. Each year, Houghton Mifflin Co. publishes an anthology called *The Best American Travel Writing*. Read some of these pieces for examples of how to tell a good travel story. Also take a look at the writing of Bill Bryson, whose highly personal tales of the Appalachian Trail, Australia, Africa and other places wonderfully blend information with humor.

- **Historical.** Every place has history for you to write about. Find the story behind those statues, buildings, and museums. Who was that man for whom everything seems to be named? Was the town rebuilt after a disaster such as a fire or flood?

• **Opinion.** Why is Paris overrated? Why are American travelers in such a hurry? Why should people ride the train instead of airplanes, or vice versa? I wrote an opinion piece about airport security practices after an incident on a trip to Los Angeles. I'll bet you can think of at least one thing from your travels that you'd like to offer your opinion about.

• **Inspirational.** Has an experience or a place you visited given you newfound insight? Did you visit the Holy Land or find solace at the Grotto in Portland, Oregon? Did an experience close to home or far away open your eyes to new ideas or possibilities? These can be specifically religious–"How I spoke to the Blessed Mother at Fatima"–or simply uplifting–"How I gained new perspective from the top of Mt. Shasta."

• **Investigative.** Are we getting ripped off by people in the travel industry? Are Americans disappearing in foreign countries? Are the airlines safe? Use your imagination for ideas, then back it up with extensive research.

• **Roundups.** Best places to eat apple pie, best ski resorts, places to see stained glass, white river rafting trips, etc.

• **Reviews**. You can review resorts, tours, hotels, restaurants, cruises, rental cars, and more.

• **Humor.** If you look at it right, there is humor in everything. Tell us the funny things that happened on your trip or the ordinary occurrences that struck you funny.

That's the just the beginning of the possibilities. In fact, you don't even have to go anywhere. If you don't have time to go very far for very long, seek stories in a circle around where you live. The very things you take for granted may be exciting story leads for an editor who lives somewhere else.

If you make a list of reasons people would want to come to your area, you can use that list to write your query, perhaps offering a story on the various things one could do in a weekend. You could also write a separate article about each activity.

Likewise, don't limit your travel articles to general-interest daily newspapers. For specialized publications, you can pursue related subjects wherever you go. If you're writing for the *Business Journal*, for example, tell us how they do business at your destination. If you're writing for a music publication, tell us about the music scene in Germany or Australia or wherever you go. For all sorts of publications, wouldn't people like to read about wine, cuisine, fashion, architecture and fascinating characters?

Nor does your story have to be an epic. Many publications run short travel items—just a few paragraphs—on various subjects, with or without photographs.

Keep the seasons in mind as you work on travel story ideas. Summer weather inspires articles on white-water rafting, camping, and fishing while winter brings thoughts of skiing, the holidays, and shopping.

Think of annual events that you could center a story on—Christmas lights, a garlic festival, a May Day celebration, the opening of deer hunting or trout fishing season, spring wildflowers, the return of the swallows.

An anniversary or a news angle can also add interest. For example, how about a return to Vietnam forty years after the war ended or a trip to Europe looking at changes since the European union and the institution of the Euro as common currency? Submit your queries as early as possible so that when the editor plans her sections, she already has you and your story in mind.

When you're traveling, take notes all along the way. The impressions will fade as soon as you head for the next location and will disappear altogether once you get home and face the realities of everyday life. Be specific. What color was it, what brand, what did that sign say that made you laugh so hard? Don't trust your memory. Describe it into a voice recorder or write it down. If you can craft actual sections of the story, even a few sentences or paragraphs to use later, you come home way ahead. If you are using a laptop and worry about somehow losing your work during the trip, e-mail your writing to yourself. It will be waiting in your inbox when you get home.

Take as many pictures as you can. Art is particularly important for travel articles. You are there; the staff is not, so shoot lots of pictures. Not only will they dress up your story, but they will bring back memories of what you saw and experienced.

Remember that you are the eyes, ears, nose, and feet of the readers. Take them along on your journey with specific imagery, colorful metaphors, and active language. A good travel article often reads like a fiction story–except that it's true.

Columns

As we've discussed, there are all kinds of newspaper articles. A column can actually be any of these. What makes it a "column" is that it appears regularly, either by the same writer every time or by different writers. It's always there, same place, same length, same format. Frankly, we all want to be columnists. And why not? Once established, it's a regular job which can build name recognition and might even lead to speaking engagements, books, fame, and fortune.

Most of us recognize humor columnist Dave Barry and a number of advice columnists, the best known one being "Dear Abby," but there are lots of other kinds of columns, including automotive, business, family, computers, food and wine, health, fitness and beauty, hobbies, home decorating, humor, political, religion, travel, opinion, and reviews. They come in different formats: question and answer, lists of tips or resources, interview, personal experience, how-to, and more.

What do you enjoy reading? What do you enjoy writing? What type of column would you like to see that doesn't seem to exist? Do you have expertise that you would like to share with readers on a weekly or monthly basis? What fascinates you? The best columns cover things you really care about.

It's a good idea to try a few short pieces on the subject before committing to an ongoing column. After writing one or two columns, you may realize that's all you have to say on that topic. Or you may discover that you have just begun to explore the subject and look forward to writing many more columns.

In order to sell a column or to write one effectively, you need a clear statement of what this column is about. *And it does have to be about something.* Lots of us want to write miscellaneous tales from our lives, but that simply won't sell. The most effective columns can be summed up in a catchy title and a few lines that everyone understands. There needs to be an audience. Who would read it? And it needs to be unique, either in subject or in the way you approach it. Just as you should be wary of committing time and energy to an ongoing column that you might lose interest in, editors are reluctant to commit precious space to a column that readers might not like or that might flop after a month. They also will be concerned that you will tire of the project and quit writing it. It will be up to you to prove that you can attract readers and keep the column going.

To be honest, columns are a hard sell. Jimmy Boegle, editor of the *Tucson Weekly,* put it well when asked if he is open to new columns: "If something is so amazing that it knocks my socks off, yes. However, given that we have no space or budget for ongoing features, and given I can't remember the last time something knocked my socks off, probably not."

Then again, Sue Harrison, arts editor of the *Provincetown Banner,* says that although she rarely accepts new columns, one of her regular freelancers recently pitched her a column about new DVDs and she bought it.

If your column interests a wide audience, you can offer it to lots of different newspapers, thereby increasing your odds and allowing you to charge less. Say you received only $10 for a 500-word column, but it ran in forty newspapers. That would pay you $400 for writing 500 words. If you wrote it weekly, your annual income from the column would be more than $20,000. While this may not be enough to quit your day job, add to this the name recognition and additional writing assignments a column would likely afford and writing a column begins to look pretty attractive.

All you have to do is hit the right places with the right idea. In other words, knock their socks off.

Other Types of Newspaper Articles

Human Interest Stories

Everybody has a story, including lots of ordinary people who don't make the front page. Many of those stories are upbeat, heart-warming antidotes to the doom and gloom that usually dominates the news. The quadriplegic who spends his days helping other people with disabilities, the 90-year-old who volunteers to help children learn to read, the couple who waited thirty years to get together—these all make good stories. And contrary to popular opinion, good news can get published.

Business Features

These are big in local papers, partially because they help sell advertising, but they also let the community know what's available. Look for a news peg, a reason to write about the business now, such as the business just opening, selling a new product, moving to a new location, or planning to close. Maybe your favorite lunch place is about to start serving dinner or just hired a new chef. Time for a story.

Personal Experience Articles

These appear in many feature sections. Here, using the first person "I," tell of something that happened to you, giving details to help the reader experience what you have experienced, using sights, sounds, smells, colors, moods and physical description. A news peg helps. For example, your experience as a shopping mall Santa Claus would be perfect for the feature section in December. Perhaps the economy hit you personally with a layoff, causing you to lose your home or to apply for food stamps. Maybe you narrowly escaped a tornado with nothing but a cat and a candy bar, or just returned from six months in Iraq. Your story might be something more ordinary, like a special moment with a child or an experience that inspired you or changed your mind about something. To interest an editor, find a way to relate your story to a larger issue beyond your own experience.

Home and Garden Stories

Weekly garden sections often use a lot of freelance work. Like business features, they attract advertising, but they also offer useful information to help readers deal with everything from remodeling their houses to mulching their rose gardens. Many are how-to's, but these sections also run features on spectacular gardens, unique use of antiques or other items in gardens, and unusual experiences with birds, raccoons, and other backyard visitors.

Investigative Articles

Want to be a private eye? These articles delve into a subject, often something in the news, ferreting out information that has not been made public before. These require a lot of work, using multiple sources to go below the surface and tell a complete story. They may unmask government wrongdoing, expose a health issue, or look into a crime or disaster.

Not long ago, gay marriage was a hot topic, especially in Oregon, where over a thousand couples were officially married. Later their marriages were ruled invalid. One has to wonder why Oregon ever let anyone get married without making sure the marriages would be legal and how this situation has affected people's lives. This could be the basis for an investigative story. At most newspapers, staff writers do the investigative pieces, but it is possible in some markets for freelancers to contribute. New American Media, a syndicate which specializes in investigative journalism, is one outlet to consider.

Newspaper Stringers

The term stringer comes from the old custom of using a string to measure the number of inches a writer should get paid for.

News Stories

News events are usually covered by staff and wire services on large newspapers, but there are many opportunities for freelancers, especially at small community newspapers or in local sections of major newspapers which hire stringers to cover city council, school board, special events, and other news.

In many cases, you'll have less than twenty-four hours to attend the event and write the story. Use the inverted pyramid style, putting the most important information in the first couple of paragraphs, working your way down to the least important facts. It's not easy, but it is exciting to be there when news is happening and be able to present it to the readers right away.

Excercises

• For an op-ed piece, free-write for twenty minutes about something that makes you angry, happy or frustrated. You probably won't have to reach very far into your brain to find something that makes you grit your teeth. Is the traffic getting to you? Are you fed up with the president—or with people criticizing the president? Are you frustrated with the lack of resources in your children's school? Is the low-carb diet obsession a conspiracy by the food industry? Should there be a constitutional amendment passed outlawing one thing or another? Why are celebrities who have no talent so popular?

Let your words flow freely. Don't worry about spelling or writing perfectly crafted sentences or even about making sense. Just write. You can go back and polish your piece before submitting it to a paper, but the emotions that pour out in your first draft will be the fire that gives it power.

• Brainstorm ideas for a column that you might write. Then try to come up with ten separate topics that you would cover. Describe each topic in a sentence or two. If you find that you have more than enough ideas, perhaps you have a column worth proposing to a newspaper. If you get stuck after two columns, maybe you'd be better off selling them as separate articles.

• Look through your daily newspaper and pick out the three sections that you find the most interesting. Then brainstorm ideas for those sections. For a real challenge, take one basic subject, such as dogs, and come up with ideas that would fit each of the different sections. For example, you could write about canine agility competitions for the sports section, homemade dog chow for the food section, and guide dogs for the living section.

Chapter 4

Queries: Pitching Your Stories

By now, you have some markets in mind and some great article ideas. It's time to talk about how to present them to editors.

Talk to ten different writers and you'll get ten different opinions on the best way to approach an editor for whom you have never written. One person says to just call the editor and ask if she's interested. Another sees no reason you shouldn't just walk into the office, samples in hand, and ask for an assignment. The third insists it is best to mail one's resume, clips, and a query letter. "No, no," says another, "you'll spend a fortune on photocopies and never hear a word. Send an e-mail."

Which is correct? Although every one of these approaches might work if you happen to offer an editor a fabulous idea that exactly fits what she's looking for, don't count on it.

"Please don't call me out of the blue," is a common refrain from editors. "Oh, heavens no," gasped one when I asked if he would like writers he'd never worked with to drop in at his office. Editors are too busy to stop everything to listen to your ideas, and even if they weren't, they couldn't say yes or no without seeing something in writing. What most want to see, depending on the type of article, is either a completed manuscript or a query letter with samples of your work.

"If you call me and pitch me something, even if I'm interested in it, I'm going to tell you to send me an e-mail because I need to see it,

I need to read it, I need to be able to think about it. If I don't have something in front of me, it's going to fade," *L.A. Times* editor David L. Ulin says. "Also the advantage of e-mail is I can read it when I'm ready, whereas with a phone call, sometimes it's a good moment and sometimes it's not a good moment."

What's a Query?

In the freelance writing business, a query letter—often referred to as simply "a query" or a "pitch"—is one of the most important things you will write because it will determine whether or not you get an assignment.

A query is a question and a proposal. The question is this: Are you interested in my idea? The proposal is: Would you like me to write it? It takes the form of a one-page letter that summarizes your idea and tells the editor why you're qualified to write the story.

You could write the whole article and send that in to see if an editor wanted it, but for most articles, editors would rather see a query first. And, if the article is rejected, you will have wasted your time. A query benefits both you and the editor because it allows you to agree on an assignment before you do the work.

You may discover that the editor wants a completely different slant than you had intended. "Run your idea by me first before you sink a lot of work into it," cautions Brad Tyer of the *Missoula Independent.*

Editors often prefer to have a hand in shaping the piece. They can tell you how long it should be, the format they prefer, and any sources they would like you to consult. They can tie it in with photos or other art. If you send a finished piece without their input, it may be a great story, but it might not be what they need at that time. In addition, having a firm assignment will give you more credibility when contacting sources as you research your story.

Preparing to Write the Query

Before you write a query, you need to have a general idea of the main points you will cover in your article. You also need to have honed your topic from a general subject, such as global warming, to a specific focus, such as how a growing shortage of snow is putting local ski resorts out of business.

You needn't do all the research in advance or write the whole piece, but you do need to know what you will be looking for and where you will find it. Stephen Buel of *East Bay Express* won't assign a story unless the writer has already made contact with the key sources and knows he can get the information he needs. The same rule applies to staff writers as well as freelancers, he says.

Of course you should also make sure you're sending your query to the right place. "Don't pitch without learning at least the basic info about the publication to which you're pitching," suggests Jimmy Boegle of the *Tucson Weekly*. "Pitch to a specific section or feature. Research, if possible, to see if we've already covered what you're pitching. If a reporter can perform these basic acts of research and reporting, it makes them look good. If not, they look very, very bad."

Once you have decided which newspaper to approach, you need the name of the editor. You should be able to find it in the newspaper, assuming you have a copy. Editors' names are usually listed in the masthead or on the editorial page. Editors of various sections are identified with a notice somewhere that tells readers where to send comments, letters, etc., or perhaps their bylines will say something like, "Tom Smith, business editor." You may find a list of editors somewhere on the newspaper's website, but sometimes all you can find is "editor@newspaper.com." That's not enough. You need an actual name and title, even if you're sending an e-mail.

If you start with "Dear Editor," or "Hi," instead of "Dear Mr. or Ms. [Editor-name]," it will be obvious that you were too lazy to find the correct name and laziness isn't an endearing quality to an editor.

If you can't find the name anywhere else, or you aren't sure if the name you have is up to date, telephone the newspaper office and ask. While you're on the line, double-check the spelling, the editor's title, and the preferred e-mail or postal address.

If you are not sure whether the editor is a man or a woman because the first name works for both, e.g., Terry or Dana, either call and ask or use both names: Dear Dana Smith.

Getting an editor's name wrong is a strike against you, and who wants to start out one strike down?

Magazines and newspapers are different in many ways, but the queries you write for them are virtually identical. And, although there are technical differences between queries you send through the postal service and queries you send by e-mail, the ingredients are the same. It's like corn muffins and corn bread. You start with the same cornmeal, flour, sugar, and milk, but muffin batter is divided into little cups in a muffin tin while corn bread batter is poured from the bowl into a square pan.

Your query is your introduction to yourself. Once the editor knows you and your work, you probably won't have to write queries at all. You can pitch your idea over the telephone or in a brief e-mail. But when you approach a new market, your query is your passport.

Recipe for a Query

The body of your query should contain three sections:

- The lead
- An overview of the article
- Your qualifications to write the piece

It should all fit on one page or the e-mail equivalent of one page. That's not as easy as it looks. You will be tempted to go on for a several pages, but don't. Busy editors appreciate a writer who can boil a query down to its essence.

The Lead

This is just like a lead to an article. You need a first paragraph that grabs the editor's interest. It might be a quote, a question, an anecdote or a startling fact.

Here are some ideas:

- When the doctor told him he'd have to amputate both legs, Josh Brannigan wanted to die...

- By the year 2010, DVDs will have gone the way of LPs and 8-track tapes.
- Dr. John Q. Smith claims to have perfected a vaccine that prevents colds.
- What do Monarch butterflies wintering in Mexico have to do with...
- I thought Mt. Hood was all about skiing until my cousin dragged me there in the middle of July.
- Most visitors to Oahu miss the best part. There's more to the island than Diamondhead and the Polynesian Cultural Center.
- Exercise is bad for you.

Writing good leads is fun and since the lead is important, spend some time on it. You might wind up using the same first paragraph for your article.

The Overview

After your lead, you must segue into what you wish to write about. It is here you will explain what you plan to write, how you plan to approach the subject and in what depth. You might start that with something like, "Would you be interested in an article on [subject] for the [section of the paper]? I plan to approach this topic..."

Here's where you outline the topics you will cover in your article and the

> ## Succinct Advice
>
> In their guidelines, the editors of South Carolina's *Free Times* urge writers to explain their ideas, give a taste of their style and tell why the topic is timely. "Assume we have no knowledge of what you're talking about. We might not." This is good succinct advice.

sources you will use. For the vaccine story, it might include some background on what causes colds, traditional treatments, who this miracle doctor is, and what others in the medical profession think about his vaccine. Explain that you will interview the doctor, get a quote from the American Medical Association, talk to people at the clinic where he practices, and interview some patients.

For the Oahu story, you might list places to go that aren't in the guidebooks, explaining that you found them on your own recent trip to the islands. You might say you will supplement your observations with research and information from people you met in Hawaii.

I often put my subtopics into a bulleted list rather than trying to write them in paragraphs. It's easier and takes less space. But it depends on the story. The Hawaii article would be perfect for this, with one bulleted item for each of the ways to have more fun in Oahu. Some story summaries flow better as paragraphs.

In your overview, it's often beneficial to give your story a headline, even though it may not be the headline that gets published in the end. A headline works as a tool for you and the editor to use when discussing your article. If it's short and catchy, it will be easier to remember.

Heads, sometimes written as "heds" in newspaper shorthand, are usually present tense and omit articles such as *a, an* and *the.* Your headline should have a strong verb. How about: "Rare Snowstorm Wallops Miami?" Subject, verb, object. Story told. "New Vaccine Prevents Colds" makes it pretty clear what this story is going to be about.

Unless the story is a very serious one, humor and puns in headlines are welcome. Alliteration—repeating the same sounds—is also good. To make it easier, you can always write a short headline that gets folks' attention, then add a subhead that offers more information. For example, headline: *River Rots*; subhead: *Mississippi River Pollution Reaching Record Levels.*

Now that you've stated what you're up to, tell the editor why his readers would be interested in this story or how they would benefit from reading it.

Here are a couple of examples:

• Your readers may suffer fewer bouts from the common cold thanks to the efforts of Dr. John Q. Smith, who claims to have perfected a vaccine that prevents colds.

- Of the 11,000 locals who will fly to Oahu this year, many will focus their visit on Diamond Head and the Polynesian. Cultural Center, missing some of the true joys of the island.

If you will provide photographs or have ideas for photos, charts or other material that can run with the article, mention it here. As we have discussed, good art can sell the story.

This is also your chance to suggest a sidebar, which is a bit of copy, usually displayed in a box, that offers information peripheral to the story. This might include a resource list, an anecdote, or a bit of other information that doesn't fit into the main story. The box titled "Succinct Advice" on page 56 of this book is a sidebar. Editors like sidebars, and they appreciate writers who offer to do them.

Your Qualifications

In this paragraph, tell the editor why you are qualified to write this article. The editor does not need the whole story of your life. She doesn't care how old you are, whether you are married, or where you went to school, unless these are pertinent to the story. She does need to know where you have been published before and/or any special knowledge you have about the subject. If you have ever had any positive contact with this newspaper before, even if it's just a letter to the editor that got published, mention it. In addition, list other publications for which you have written. If this is a long list, just mention the most important credits or the ones most closely related to your topic.

New writers who don't have many—or any—publication credits need to seek credibility in other ways. Your life experiences, your job history, or your hobbies can all help show the editor that you know what you're talking about. A paragraph explaining what got you interested in the subject may do the job. If you have tried the new cold vaccine, say so. If you used to lead tours in Hawaii, definitely include that. Likewise, if you're writing for a parenting newspaper and you have children, or if you want to write music reviews and you have a degree in music, tell the editor.

Sometimes writers are tempted to slip their résumés in with their clips. Don't. Most editors aren't interested in every job you ever had. If they do want a résumé, they'll let you know.

That's it. Conclude with something like: I look forward to hearing from you.

Submitting Your Query

Not long ago, all queries traveled on paper by mail. Some still do, especially for magazine articles and book proposals. But these days the newspaper business depends on e-mail for almost all communication. "E-mail rules. We take no freelance in hard copy," says June Wormsley, travel editor of the *San Antonio Express News.* Of the editors surveyed, only two preferred submissions by mail. And nobody wanted them by fax. Queries sent by fax get mixed up with the ad proofs, press releases and interoffice memos and often don't make it to the editor's desk.

E-mail makes it easier for the writer, too. Whether you live across the street or across the country, you can submit queries, articles and photos, and communicate with editors almost as easily as if you were in the same building. E-mail is also great for interviewing sources.

Later in this chapter, we will discuss how to prepare paper submissions, but these days, if you're looking for a newspaper assignment, try e-mail first unless the newspaper's guidelines tell you otherwise.

Formatting the E-Mail Query

Just because you send a query by e-mail doesn't mean you get to be chatty and informal. You should work as hard and give the same information in an e-query as in one that travels by snail mail. Write your query in your word processing program, revising and polishing with the same care as you would use for an article. When it's perfect, you can paste it into an e-mail.

Address your e-mail directly to the editor of the section you're aiming for, and make sure it does not look like junk mail. Editors receive hundreds of e-mails a day. Use the subject heading to make it clear that this is a query, not spam, not a press release, and not a "letter to the editor." Mention your topic in a word or two, as in "Query: Llama competition."

Make sure your own e-mail address sounds professional. A query from foxychick@yahoo.com is likely to be dismissed. Even if it's clearly marked as a query, an editor may wonder how professional you really are. It's easy to obtain a second e-mail address for business use. Many companies offer them for free. Probably the best e-mail moniker is simply a variation of your name so the recipient knows who you are.

If you are sending e-queries to more than one publication, send separate e-mails to each one. An editor who opens a letter with the addresses of several publications at the top is likely to hit *delete* so hard she breaks a fingernail. You could use the BCC or blind carbon copy function, but that would not allow you to tailor your query to each specific publication, and no editor wants to receive the same pitch as everybody else.

Unless the newspaper's guidelines direct you to do otherwise, paste your query into the body of your e-mail. Do not send attachments until requested to do so. Most editors will not open attachments from people they don't know. Once you have the assignment, they might want you to send the finished article as an attachment.

With e-mail submissions, don't indent the first lines of your paragraphs. Instead, type them flush left and leave a space between paragraphs. If you use quotation marks, go into the tools menu of your word processing program and turn off the "smart quotes" feature. Otherwise, your quotes may come out as odd symbols. Also, stick to black print and avoid any fancy formatting, such as boldface or italics, which may be lost in the e-mail process.

Whether or not the editor's name is part of the e-mail address, address the editor with his honorific and name just as you would with a letter. Then go into the body of your query.

Although the e-mail program will automatically put your name and the date on the message, type in your name, address, phone number and e-mail address underneath your query, so that the editor will know how to reach you. If you have a website, include that address, too, so the editor can find out more about you.

Now, stop a minute. Check and double-check what you have written. It is easy to hit the send button and later discover that you left something out or made an error.

Querying the Old-Fashioned Way

Some editors still want paper queries. I understand the desire to have your letter stand out from the big stack the editor has to read every day, but I urge you to make yours the most tasteful rather than the most flashy. Black print in standard 12-point type on a classy white, cream, tan or gray stationery will make a good first impression. Also resist the urge to try out unusual type fonts or emblazon the word WRITER across the top in 48-point type.

Office supply stores sell all kinds of eye catching stationery in various colors, with designs ranging from mountains to trees to butterflies. Save these for your personal correspondence.

You could have a letterhead made at a print shop, but you can just as easily create your own on your computer. I keep a file on my hard drive called "Letterhead." When I want to write a letter, I open that file, copy the heading and paste it into my document. It starts my letter off with a professional look and gives all the basic information.

Your letterhead should include your name, address, telephone number, fax number if you have one, and e-mail address. Make it easy for the editor to contact you. If the answer to your query is yes, particularly on a time-sensitive story, she may want to assign the story as quickly as possible.

What your query says is more important than the format in which it is written. Editors do not obsess over whether the margins of your query are exactly one inch wide, whether you put one or two spaces between the date and the address, or whether you indent the paragraphs. They don't care. They just want the information presented neatly and clearly, but they do expect some resemblance to a standard business letter. Format your query like a business letter, single spacing and using a business-like font.

If you are sending a query by mail, always include a self-addressed, stamped envelope (SASE) for a response. If they aren't interested in what you are pitching, most editors will not reply without an SASE. Replies, even rejections, are valuable. At least you know the editor saw the query and since editors are, well, editors, some can't resist scribbling notes or other helpful information on the query before returning it.

Of course, if an editor is interested, the SASE isn't likely to be used. In my experience, rejections come in the mail and acceptances arrive by telephone or e-mail. As an editor, when I saw a query for a story that I wanted, I was usually in a hurry to finalize the story, and made a phone call. Still, include an SASE. It might come back to you with a contract, a note from the editor, updated guidelines, or simply your clips ready to go on to a new editor.

If you are mailing your work to a country outside the United States, don't put U.S. postage on the return envelope. Purchase International Reply Coupons from the post office instead.

While we're on the subject of mailing, first class postage is usually sufficient. Remember, if you're using an envelope that is bigger than a standard business envelope, you need at least two stamps. Buy yourself a postal scale or go to the post office to get an accurate fix on how much postage is needed. There is no logical reason to send your query—or even your manuscript—by registered mail, express mail or any other more expensive method unless your material is extremely time-sensitive. Don't annoy the editor by requiring her to sign a paper saying she received your query.

Punctuation Primer

Period: Place where you want a reader to come to a complete stop.

Exclamation point: Use extremely sparingly. Bonnie Hearn Hill (BonnieHillHearn.com), a writer and teacher of note, says, "You only get six exclamation points in your lifetime. Use them wisely."

Comma: used to identify a modifying word or phrase, to mark a series, or to indicate a pause. Here are more specific rules for when to use commas:

To separate items listed in a series: apples, oranges, peaches, and pears.

To introduce dialogue: He said, "I'm tired."

When you turn around a sentence and start with a dependent clause: Yesterday, it rained. Because he didn't study, he failed the exam.

To set off a person's name when being spoken to or identified after another word: "Mark, why are you so late?" "My son, Peter, is a genius."

To avoid confusion with multiple clauses.

For parenthetic expressions: Sam, who is from Portland, is an architect.

Before the word "but" when it begins a separate clause: "I wanted to go, but I had the flu."

Semicolon: halfway between a comma and a period. A longer stop, but not as final as a period. "God creates; man destroys." Also used in a long series to avoid confusion.

Colon: a dramatic pause or to introduce a list or series: There was only one thing left to do: go home. If the material after the colon forms a complete sentence, start with a capital letter.

Dash: sudden or sharp break in the thought or flow of the sentence—typed with two hyphens thus: --. Some word-processing programs offer an automatic "em dash," but if you are sending your work over the Internet, it may come out as gibberish.

Hyphen: for dividing words or making compound words.

Parentheses: set off material that would disrupt the sentence.

Quotation marks: used for short titles and quoted material. Use at the beginning and end of the speech. In a long speech extending through several paragraphs, use quotes at the beginning of each paragraph and at the end of only the last one.

Note: In most newspapers, commas and periods *always* go inside the quotation marks, even if the quotes are around a title.

Ellipsis: Use three periods to indicate that words have been left out of a quotation. If it comes at the end of a sentence, type the three dots and a period to mark the end of the sentence. Four periods total.

Clips and other Enclosures

Sending samples of your work or clips with your query increases your chances. This part is easier with snail mail submissions because you can enclose photocopies of your published articles.

Experts vary on how many clips to send. Some say one is enough, while others rcommend five. I usually send three. The idea is to give editors a representative sample while not overloading them with your complete work. If possible, send clips on a related subject. For example, if you're doing a query for a story about a disease and you previously wrote about measles, that's the clip to send, not the feature on the rodeo clown.

Don't send an original clip straight out of the newspaper; a photocopy is fine. When you have something published that you are proud of, make several copies. Then when you need a clip, you can pull it out of the file quickly. I have heard of writers going to great lengths to arrange clips artistically on a page. Don't bother. Just photocopy the story. If the date and name of the publication aren't on the clip, write them in neatly with a pen. Again, editors care more about the content than the format.

Send your best work. Editors are aware that published articles have been edited. For all they know, they have been completely rewritten, but it gives them something to go on.

You might also have e-clips, stories that can be accessed on the Internet. If you have published online or if a publication you have written for archives its stories at its website, you can definitely include these as clips. If you are sending a snail mail query, print out a copy and include it, rather than asking the editor to find it online.

For an e-mail query, include links to your online clips. Do not add the clips to your query letter as attachments. Not only are editors nervous about viruses, but they may not be able to read attachments in various formats. If you have online clips, just give them the web addresses or provide live links that will take them to your stories. Again, these should be your best work, not chosen simply because they happen to be available in digital form.

If all of your clips are on paper, you have two options with an e-query. You can either scan the stories into the computer or put them into an Adobe Acrobat PDF document and send them with your e-mail (pasted in or as links), or simply offer to mail them upon request. If your query sounds promising, the editor will be willing to wait a few days for the mail to see your clips.

A Few More Query Points

Attitude is important in a query. You want to sound confident without sounding cocky. Avoid begging, bragging or apologizing. If you have never published anything, don't mention it. If you are unsure about any part of your story, either don't send the query until you are sure or keep your doubts to yourself. Don't say you'll be happy to do a rewrite; that tells the editor you don't have any faith in your abilities. At the same time, do not write that this is the best story idea anyone has ever seen, that it should go on page one. If your idea is good, the editor will recognize it.

Also, don't mention money at this point. It will just turn the editor off. You can deal with the money issue later.

One more big thing: Check, double-check and triple-check your queries for spelling and grammar errors and typos. Don't assume that your computer's spelling and grammar checkers will catch everything. They won't, especially when you type something that is a real word but not the word you intended. Set your query aside for at least a day, then reread it carefully. If you have any doubts, ask someone else to read it before you send it out. If an editor sees mistakes in your query, she will wonder how accurate your article will be. Make your query perfect.

Sample Query Letters

Below is a successful e-query I sent to the editor of *HOMEBusiness Journal,* for whom I had written three previous articles. Unfortunately, this great outlet for freelancers has gone out of business.

Dear Kim:

Although most of us know mushrooms as the knobby white things we buy at the grocery store, Marjie Millard knows that there's a lot more to mushrooms than what's offered at the local Safeway.

Millard started making money picking mushrooms in the 1980s, following the seasons around the Pacific Northwest. Shortly after she settled in Waldport on the Central Oregon Coast, she started her own business, Millard Family Mushrooms. With occasional help from her children, ages 12 and 14, she picks and sells many varieties of mushrooms, including Black Trumpet Chanterelles, Candy Caps, Cauliflowers, Hedgehogs, Lobsters, Chicken of the Woods, Morels, King Boletes and Matsutakes. She offers some of her crop fresh at local farmers' markets. The rest she dries and packages in her kitchen for restaurants and individual customers all over the country. Some of the mushrooms go into a pre-packaged soup mixture that she also sells.

I would love to write an article about Marjie's Millard Family Mushrooms for *HOMEBusiness Journal.* I can provide photos, if you'd like. It's an unusual business, based on a product which grows naturally in this rain-soaked area. Millard is talkative, attractive and energetic. She is active in the local mushroom society and plays a big role in the annual mushroom festival, held every October.

I am pleased to have written several articles in the past year for *HOMEBusiness Journal,* most recently the piece on buying a new computer. I think your readers would enjoy this one.

Let me know what you think. FYI, mushrooms are most plentiful around here between September and December, so it would be good to do the interview and photos during the next few months.

Sincerely,
Sue Fagalde Lick

Here's a sample snail mail query:

SUE FAGALDE LICK
[address]
South Beach, OR 97366
email:suelick@casco.net

March 1, 2006

Kay Balmer, editor
Homes and Gardens section
The Oregonian
1320 SW Broadway
Portland, OR 97201

Dear Ms. Balmer:

What could be more luxurious after a long day than soaking in a spa until your skin is red and you're so sleepy you can barely stay awake? It's like a giant bathtub, only bigger and hotter, and you can look at the stars while you soak. But is it safe?

Our house came with a hot tub. At first we used it daily, but we began to wonder if that overheated, slightly woozy feeling is a good thing. We had trouble getting the chemistry right. If the pH is bad for the Fiberglass surface, what will it do to our skin? Should we use the spa when we're sick? We soon had more questions than answers. I would like to explore the safety aspects of regular hot tub use in an article you might title "Spa Shock." The questions I will answer with the help of spa experts and health professionals include:

- How hot is too hot?
- How do you know when it's time to get out?
- Should you use the spa when you're sick or injured?
- Most people have heard that pregnant women

and people with heart problems should not use a spa, but what other conditions put one at risk?

    • Are the chemicals we put in the water safe for repeated exposures? If the pH or the chlorine is off, will it hurt us?

    • Can a person become addicted to the feeling of hot, hot, hot water?

In over thirty years as a professional writer and editor, I have published three non-fiction books, worked on several California and Oregon newspapers, and sold freelance articles to many publications. While living in San Jose, I was a regular contributor to *Bay Area Homestyle* and wrote for the Metro newspaper chain's home and garden sections.

Say the word and I'll get started.

Sincerely,
Sue Fagalde Lick

Cover Letters

For some types of articles, there's no point in writing a query letter because you have already written the whole thing. This is especially true for columns, humor, and opinion pieces, the sorts of things an editor can't judge until they are complete. For these, you need to enclose a cover letter with the completed work. This letter should be short, only two or three paragraphs that explain what this is and who you are. A half page is usually enough. Beyond that, the work needs to speak for itself.

Catch the editor's attention with an engaging opening sentence. Then, in one paragraph, tell the editor what you are sending, how long it is and where you think it might fit in the newspaper. Include another paragraph on who you are, what you have published before and, if relevant, what your inspiration for this piece was. That's it.

Keep your cover letter business-like. Later on, if you establish a relationship with an editor, you may be able to scrawl a handwritten note to him, using first names and minimal information, but for now, this is a formal introduction to you and your work. Keep it professional.

The same applies if you are sending a story by e-mail. No happy faces.

Don't forget to include your contact information.

Mail the letter with your manuscript (see Chapter 7 for manuscript formatting guidelines) or send an e-mail that begins with the cover letter, followed by the pasted-in article. Again, don't send e-mail attachments unless they have been requested.

Sample Cover Letter

This cover letter was included with my successful e-mail submission to a paper called *Skirt!*, which is published both in print and online.

Dear Ms. Hardin:

If we were really honest, most people would admit that, except for the sex, we'd rather have the whole bed to ourselves. That's the idea behind my essay "The Truth About Double Beds," which I hope you will consider publishing in *Skirt!* I found your site through Writersweekly.com, and I love it. The story is pasted below.

I have been a professional writer for 30 years, working as a staff reporter and editor for newspapers in California and Oregon before I began freelancing full-time. My articles have appeared in *The Oregonian, Bay Area Parent, Portuguese Heritage Journal,* and *Oregon Coast,* among others.

I look forward to hearing from you soon.

Sincerely,

Sue Fagalde Lick
(mailing address)
(telephone)
(e-mail address)

Getting the Editor's Attention

You have written a brilliant query, mailed it to the proper editor and heard absolutely nothing. While there is usually a lag time between mailing and response with freelance submissions to any type of publication, editors at newspapers (and everywhere else) are notorious for the time it takes for them to respond or make no response at all. This applies to e-mail queries as much as snail mail queries. Just because you can send your submission instantly doesn't mean they will reply instantly.

The delay goes back to the extreme workload most editors face and the fact that papers and e-mail messages pile up faster than anyone can keep track of. That means if your query or manuscript arrives while an editor is on deadline, he probably won't see it for a few days. By then, it might be buried under an avalanche of letters, faxes and e-mails. This means you, the writer, need to be gently proactive.

"Everybody's completely overworked," David L. Ulin says. "So when an editor doesn't get back to you, or you don't get a response right away, or even sometimes you don't get a response at all, it's not because they're sending you a message; it's because your e-mail got lost in the pile." Ulin says he has found e-mails from weeks earlier that simply slipped by. It's okay for a writer to send another e-mail politely asking if a decision has been made, he says.

With magazine submissions, it's important to wait through the response time they state in their guidelines, whether it's two months or six months or even longer, then send a letter, but if you do that with newspapers, you may never hear anything. Also, your story may need to be written right away, before it goes out of date. Give them a week or two, then contact the editor. You can save yourself some stress by sending your query or article well ahead of any related event. Most editors of daily or weekly newspapers want to receive queries a month or more before publication and completed articles at least two weeks in advance. For monthlies, think farther ahead. Your article may be due a whole month before the issue is published.

I cannot state strongly enough that editors cannot deal with you or me or anyone else while they're on deadline trying to finish their own writing, edit stories and figure out the puzzle that is every issue of the newspaper. Some editors won't take telephone calls, even from their families, while they're on deadline.

So what's a writer to do? If you send a letter, it might get buried in the same pile as your original submission. A fax will never get to the editor. E-mail is usually the best approach. As with your e-mailed query, make sure your name and subject tip off the editor that you are a real writer asking a professional question. Remind him of what your story was about and when you sent it. Then he can look up your query or manuscript and reply when the deadline crunch is over.

Although some editors discourage writers they haven't worked with before from telephoning them, others don't mind a quick follow-up call. In fact, a phone call could open up a dialogue that leads to other things. However, do not expect the editor to remember your submission or know exactly where it is. Chances are he'll have to make a note and get back to you.

Before you call, find out the best times to talk to the editor. Usually that's shortly after the paper comes out. Then the editor is more relaxed and starting to plan the next issue. For morning dailies, editors start work in the afternoons, finishing late at night. The best time to call is early in the afternoon before the deadline crunch hits. For an afternoon paper, reverse the process. For a weekly newspaper, or for weekly sections of a daily paper, the most relaxed day is the day the paper or section comes out.

However you choose to follow up on your article, be polite. Do not whine about how long it's taking, and don't be critical of the editor. Even if you're thinking nasty thoughts, don't express them. Try to be as helpful as possible. "I mailed you a story idea about Oahu on June 3, and I was wondering if you had decided yet. I'm really anxious to get started on it." That's pretty much all you need to say, unless you have come across some new information that might sway the editor.

The editor might say she doesn't remember the story at all and will have to find it and call you back. She might say she likes it but isn't sure yet how it will fit in with other stories she's planning to run. She might tell you that she has to present her story list at the next staff meeting and that's not happening until next week. Or she might say it's just not going to work.

When the Editor Says No

If the editor rejects your idea or finished article, don't throw a hissy fit and don't try to change his mind. Take no for an answer. Say, "Thank you very much for your time." You might calmly ask what you could have done to make the idea more appealing, but don't press too hard. Sometimes it's more a gut feeling than anything specific the editor can articulate.

If you still want to write for that newspaper, submit another idea. You might even mention it while you're talking about what happened to the first idea. Chances are the editor will ask for a written query, but it wouldn't hurt to say, "I had another idea. Would you be interested in a story on…the new bakery that makes donuts without holes?"

Most of all, don't take rejections personally. Editors are rejecting the writing on the page or screen, not you. Ideas can be rejected for all kinds of reasons, most of them having nothing to do with your ability as a writer. Perhaps the paper already ran something similar or perhaps advertising sales are down and the space available for feature stories has been reduced. Maybe the publisher is tired of stories about diseases. You never know. Come up with something else. In fact, if the editor is at all encouraging, you might try sending a letter including several ideas at once. Offer a paragraph for each idea, concluding with one paragraph listing your qualifications. Just make sure that every idea is really tailored to that newspaper.

When the Editor Says Yes

If the news is good, silently do a happy dance, but don't hang up the telephone or start working on the story until you get some details straight. Always ask when it's due, how many words it should be, what format he wants you to send it in, and whether he needs you to take pictures or make suggestions for photo possibilities. Also find out when it will run because everyone you interview will want to know.

Now is the time to discuss payment. Most papers have standard fees for particular types of stories. First-timers should probably accept whatever they're offered. But once you have a little experience, try negotiating a higher rate.

If the editor happens to ask you what you charge, you risk losing the assignment if the number you give is too high or cheating yourself out of some money if it's too low. Freelancer Jennifer Meacham suggests, "Tell the editor you have a figure in mind, but want to make sure it fits within their parameters. Ask the editor what the standard range is for articles such as this. Then say, no matter what the price, 'Well, that seems a little low.'"

Ask what expenses they will cover, whether they will send you copies of the paper when it comes out, and when you will be paid. If they don't send you a contract or letter spelling these things out, send them a letter or e-mail so that you both have it in writing. You can say something like: "Thank you for the assignment to write about the Happy Hopping Llama Club. I agree to write a 1,200-word article, due Aug. 31, to be submitted by e-mail, along with suggestions for photos. I understand that I will be paid $75 on publication for first rights."

Copyright

This brings up the question of rights. In the United States, your work is automatically protected by copyright laws the instant you put the words on a page or on your computer screen. The question is how many of your rights you will sell to the newspaper. Most newspapers include a copyright notice which appears to claim the rights for the entire contents. That copyright is for that particular arrangement of materials as a whole. It does not take away your individual right to the article—unless you give it away or sell it to them.

Ideally you will give the newspaper only first serial rights or one-time rights. That means you can resell the article. Some newspapers will buy the rights to a story for a specified time, e.g., six months or a year, after which you are free to offer it to other newspapers.

Try not to sell more than one-time rights, but you won't always have a choice in the matter. In recent years, large conglomerates have been buying up local newspapers. In fact, every community newspaper I ever worked for is now part of a giant newspaper chain. These mega-media companies each own dozens of newspapers, as well as radio and TV stations, and various Internet outlets. The bigger the company, the more likely they are to insist on purchasing all rights to your story. If your contract asks you to sell them all rights—which means you can never publish it anywhere else, not even in a future book or on your website—you need to decide whether the pay and exposure are worth it. Sometimes they are. Maybe you need the clips or couldn't sell that particular story anywhere else anyway.

For some writers, the all-rights clause is a deal-breaker. Jennifer Meacham, who has written for several major dailies in the Pacific Northwest, says she recently turned down a sale she really wanted because the company would not alter its "all rights" clause. Not only did that company claim all the rights to her story, but the contract demanded that she surrender all of her notes and research materials. Because she was planning to a write a book on a related subject, she fought for her rights all the way to the owner of the company but ultimately had to walk away. "I always retain some rights, even if it's just rights to post the article on my website so editors can have access to it after the subscription period on that publication has ended."

David L. Ulin, on the other hand, says he didn't worry much about retaining resale rights on his articles when he was freelancing. To him, it wasn't worth the effort to resell his stories to other markets. "The numbers are so low when you're talking about picking up another 50 or 75 bucks. I'd also lose interest. There were other pieces I wanted to write, and I'd rather just spend my time doing that." Now, as book editor of the *L.A. Times*, which is owned by the Tribune Company, his standard contract claims all rights.

Often on smaller newspapers, the editor doesn't have a firm policy about rights and will let you keep them just for the asking. Know what you are selling. Get it in writing. If you aren't comfortable with the terms offered, try to negotiate changes, but if they won't budge, decide how badly you want to sell that story to that newspaper. Remember, there are plenty more ideas and other angles to write new stories.

While you are discussing rights, also find out if the paper is going to publish your story online as well as in print. Many papers publish everything online these days, with no additional pay. The whole subject of e-rights is far from settled, but the Internet is a whole other world of publication possibilities which you should keep as open as possible. If they are going to put your story online, suggest a time limit, after which you can publish it on other websites.

Making matters more complicated, as more and more hometown papers are purchased by large conglomerates, editors share stories, sometimes without consulting you. For example, Silicon Valley Community Newspapers, which used to be an independent operation, is now owned by the same company that owns the *San Jose Mercury News*. Although the local weeklies pay 10 cents a word and another 50 percent for stories that appear in other papers of their chain for first rights, the *Mercury News* now has access to all of their stories. If the *Merc* decides to pick up an article from the *Saratoga News*, for example, it can claim all print and online rights *for no additional pay*. Some freelancers avoid such contracts while others are so happy to gain the more impressive clips from the biggest paper in the Bay Area that they don't mind losing their rights and not getting any more money. Whatever the situation, make sure you know what rights you are selling before you accept any publication agreement.

Note: If you publish an article on your own website or blog, some publishers believe that you have used up your first online rights and will reject your story or offer less pay because the story is a reprint.

New writers often worry about having their ideas stolen by unethical editors. This does not occur very often, but it's possible. Copyright does not cover ideas, only the specific expression of those ideas. More often than direct theft, what happens is that a subject is getting a lot of publicity and other people come up with ideas that are similar to yours at the same time.

Simultaneous Submissions

Because the waiting time can drive writers crazy, many are tempted to send the same thing to several competing publications at once. There is no law against this, and the odds are against all of them wanting to buy your article. You can send your idea to as many papers as you want. Ethically, if the papers are published in the same market, you should tell them you are doing so, even though that might lessen your chances of a sale. Editors want to be the first ones with the story.

If more than one wants your piece, you could wind up with some angry editors who don't want to hear from you again.

However, you can definitely submit to more than one newspaper if they are not owned by the same company or in competition with each other. Papers that are owned by the same newspaper chain, such as Gannett or the Tribune Company, often share stories. Try not to send the same thing to different papers within the same corporate family. Pick the one closest to home and wait for its response before moving on.

You are safe offering the same story to noncompeting newspapers as long it fits their mission in some way. Newspapers published in Florida and New York may have different readers and completely different contents. Likewise, papers published for Presbyterians and Catholics or sculptors and musicians have different readers. Travel articles are particularly adaptable to multiple sales because they are not tied as tightly to the local area. Columns, how-to's, roundup pieces and features of national or international interest can be submitted to multiple publications. It is also possible to re-slant the same idea, as we discussed in the last chapter, taking the same basic facts and connecting them with a local person, place or organization or giving the story a new angle. If it's a different story, you don't have to tell anyone about the other variations. If the newspapers are in completely different markets, I wouldn't mention your multiple queries either, unless you have actually sold the article. Then you may need to give credit to the paper where it appears first.

What Went Where?

Writers who are sending queries, articles and letters out to various publications can very quickly forget what went where. It is essential to keep good records of what you send out and what the response was. I keep a folder on each query that I submit. Inside is all of my research and copies of all correspondence. I also keep a chart where I list the article or query, the market, the date I sent it out, when the piece was assigned, purchased and published, and how much I got paid.

The best system is whatever works best for you. You may want to keep all of your records on the computer. A spreadsheet works well for keeping track of what you have sent and what its status is. There are also commercial story-tracking programs, such as Writer's Market's Submission Tracker. A form which you can photocopy and use to track your submissions is included on page 166 in the resources section at the back of this book.

Good old file cards work as well as anything. In my pre-computer days, I wrote my submission information on color-coded 4- x 6-inch cards, blue for queries, yellow for publications. I marked the stories that were currently under consideration with paper clips. Later I added a pink section for columns.

Whatever system you use, keep everything. If your idea doesn't sell to the first place you send it, you'll want to try it somewhere else, and you definitely don't want to do all that work again.

The important thing is that you keep records somehow. Not only do you need to know what you have sent, especially if an editor calls with an acceptance or questions, but if you pursue writing as a business, you need records to convince the Internal Revenue Service that you are a working writer. A list of submissions and responses will go a long way toward proving you really are striving to get published (more on this later).

Exercise

• Draft an article query on one of your ideas from the exercises in the previous chapters, addressing it to one of the newspapers you selected in Chapter 1 or another market that seems likely. List what clips or supporting material you will send out with it.

Chapter 5

Researching Your Article

The prosecutor stood and addressed the judge. "Your honor, the defendant, Joe Jones, is a cold-blooded killer, and that's all I have to say."

The judge peered at him over his half-glasses. "Counselor, are you telling me you do not have any evidence to present?"

"Evidence? No, Your Honor. We don't need any evidence."

"You have no proof?"

"No, I just know that he killed Sherry Smith."

The judge banged his gavel. "Counselor, that is simply not enough. You must present evidence to prove your allegation. Case dismissed. Mr. Jones, you are free to go."

Just as evidence proves the case in the courtroom, we writers need details to prove our points. It takes facts from reliable sources and testimony by reliable witnesses to convince the reader that what we say is true. Yet too many of us are like the prosecuting attorney who tries to send a man to jail simply by saying that he's a killer.

We need solid evidence. You say she's a prize-winning artist, but what prizes has she won? List them. You write, "He's highly educated." What colleges did he attend and what degrees did he earn? Let us in on it.

You may write about a "wonderful new restaurant" but if you don't let us hear from the chef how the food is prepared or even what's on the menu, we'll have to take your word for it. These are the kinds of missing details that will force the editor to call for more information or simply to reject your story, just as the judge rejected the prosecutor's case.

It Is all about Trust

In any kind of article, you need to get across to the reader that he can trust what you say (unless it's humor, and then that should be established early).

If an editorial writer wants to convince his readers that Social Security should be scrapped in favor of a different plan, he needs to present some background on how Social Security started, how it works now, and why it needs changing. Then we need to know how this new plan will be better. A writer just stating his opinion is not going to convince anyone, but with the right combination of facts, quotations, and anecdotes, the reader might change his mind.

In a 2005 op-ed piece about pharmacists who withhold prescriptions that go against their Christian beliefs, *Miami Herald* writer Leonard Pitts didn't just give his opinion. In fact, he didn't tell us what he thought until two-thirds of the way through. First he described a situation in Illinois where pharmacists were refusing to fill prescriptions for the "morning after" pill. Then he talked about other places where this had happened and about laws that had been passed or were being considered in sixteen states. Finally he hit us with his opinion, beginning with the plainly stated, "What a crock." By the last sentence of his editorial, I completely agreed with him, but what if he had just said, "I heard that some pharmacists refuse to give prescriptions. I think they're wrong." Would I have believed him? Not likely. Back up your opinions with facts. Otherwise, as they say in the courtroom, it's just hearsay.

In journalism classes, reporters are taught to back up the facts in their stories with quotes from at least three different sources. Some editors won't consider anything less. The guidelines for *Creative Loafing Atlanta* state: "We want writers to use multiple sources and, if necessary, documents and other public records to get a full-bodied understanding of their subject. We do not accept single-source stories."

The rule of three works for all types of writing. Give me three reasons I should believe you. Be specific. Name your sources. Tell me whom you talked to, where and when the article you quote was published, or what organization was behind the research study you derived your facts from. Then I can access the same information myself if I want to.

Place Your Sources into Your Article

Newspapers don't use footnotes. Instead, the source is woven into the text. For example: "According to Joe Jones, head of the biological sciences department at Cornell University,..."

Nor do newspapers include bibliographies, but you need to attribute every statement that is not common knowledge or your own personal experience to the source where you got it. This reliance on stated sources is one of the things that separates newspaper writing from creative writing.

Major magazines employ *fact-checkers*. A fact-checker's job is to verify everything. They may ask the writer for a list of sources and sometimes even require that the writer send an annotated copy of the manuscript showing where every statement came from. This can be a headache for the writer, but fact-checkers protect writers from stupid mistakes. Most newspapers don't have any such person. Unless the editor has reason to doubt, he or she will trust what you say. If you make a serious factual error, the readers will let the editor know, and that may be the last assignment you get from that newspaper.

Just like an attorney, a writer gathers evidence from research, observation, and interviews—in other words, detective work.

The Writer's Firsthand Observation

Your own observations may yield the most convincing evidence. If you want to write a travel article about historic cemeteries, go and actually touch the gravestones. If you want to write about a local club, attend a meeting. And if you want to write about a person, spend time with him. Use all of your senses to show us what you discovered while you were there. What time of day was it? Was it dark or light, raining or sunny? What did you see? Did you see mountains, beaches, tennis courts? A room? What color? What kind of furniture was in it? Were there books, toys, cats, or shoes scattered around? What did you hear? Water running, children chattering, music playing? What kind of music? Classical music gives a very different impression from country or hip-hop.

Picture how a dog sniffs the air. What did you smell? Cookies baking? Potpourri? Air freshener? Dirty socks? Mildew? Apply your sense of touch. Was the chair you were sitting on hard or soft, smooth or scratchy? When you shook hands coming in, were the other person's fingers warm or cold, strong or limp?

Even taste can apply. Did you have coffee or wine, an Oreo cookie or fresh plums? Or was nothing offered? All of your observations are evidence that will help take the reader into the scene with you.

For a feature on a local artist go to the gallery where his work is on display and look at it. It is usually better to see the paintings and think about them on your own rather than with the artist standing next to you, talking and waiting for your reaction. Plus, studying the art will spark questions to ask the artist.

If you are writing about efforts to prepare for a tsunami, go to the beach. Observe the waves and the patterns of wet and dry sand. See for yourself where the shore is high enough above sea level to be safe and where everything in sight is likely to be inundated with water. Take notes on what you see to add color and credibility to your article.

Finding the evidence you need may require detective work, but it's worth the effort to present an airtight case. Go poke around the scene, be nosy, ask questions, write down your observations. If anyone asks, tell them you're a writer trying to get the details just right. They will appreciate your quest for accuracy.

Planning Your Research

Personal observation is important, but it's not enough. You will need to read what others have written on the subject and interview people who can provide additional information. As you are interviewing them watch for quotes you can use in the piece.

Before you hit the library or the Internet or start setting up interviews, take out a blank piece of paper or open a new file on your computer. First, list your topic. Then write down the questions you need to answer to do your story. Leave several blank spaces under each question. If you're not sure what to ask, try the old *who, what, where, when,* and *how* of traditional journalism, to which I would add *why.* They work for just about any subject.

For the feature on a local artist, you might want to ask:

- What is his complete name?
- Is he from out of the area? If so, where is he from?
- What type of art does he do?
- If this is an unusual type of art, what is it and how is it done?
- Where is his studio and what is it like?
- What is the artist's background and training?
- Why did he choose to be an artist?
- What inspires him?
- What shows has he had and what prizes has he won?
- When and where is his next show?
- What do critics and other artists say about his work?
- What does he do when he's not making art?
- What are his plans for the future?

For the article about preparing for a tsunami, you might ask:

- What exactly is a tsunami?
- How likely is it that one will occur here?
- What areas are most vulnerable?
- What plans are in place?
- How will people know if they need to evacuate?
- How does preparation in this town compare to preparation in other places?

There can be more questions, but you get the idea. Working with the same list of questions all the way from the initial idea through writing the finished article is a great help in corralling the research and producing the story. If you aren't sure what you're looking for, you won't know when to stop researching. You might gather reams of material that ultimately does not apply to your article.

In the artist story, you don't need to know about his wife, kids, or previous work experience in another field unless they apply to his art. You don't need to know where he buys his paint or other supplies or everything about the gallery where he shows his work either. In the tsunami story, if you try to learn everything about waves, earthquakes and the history of tsunamis, you will never finish. So, figure out what you need to know and focus your research.

Who Has the Answers?

The next step is to brainstorm about where you might find the answers to your questions. In the spaces under your questions, write down possible sources of information. For the artist story, the artist himself will probably answer most of your questions, but don't stop there. Visit his website. Look up articles in newspapers and art magazines to see what other people have said about him. Talk to his agent or someone at his gallery to get another point of view.

For the tsunami story, for which you will need to gather government and scientific articles and reports, check newspapers, magazines and scientific journals for what has already been written and set up interviews with government officials, rescue agencies and citizens who are working on tsunami preparedness. Look up information on past tsunamis to see what happened and what has changed since then.

From the Internet to the Library

After you have figured out what you want to know, expand your research beyond what you did to write your query. Take another look on the Internet, using the various search engines, such as Google and Yahoo. Online databases offer additional information. Some can only be accessed at the library or by paying a hefty fee, but others are free. You can read about tsunamis, for example, at the *Encyclopedia Britannica* website, and that site will direct you to other sources. Also search news groups and blogs. The phenomenal Wikipedia, a free online encyclopedia that anyone can add to, is quite handy and, according to studies done, usually quite accurate.

Be Wary

Just because someone has posted something on the Internet does not mean he knows any more about the subject than you do. Check credentials. A marine scientist with a Ph.D. from the Scripps Institution of Oceanography at the University of California San Diego probably knows more about tsunamis than some kid who has posted his opinions at Myspace.com.

Of course, since anyone can add to Wikipedia, you will have to use common sense when relying on information you glean from it. Often you can use it for background information, verifying anything suspicious.

When researching online, make your search terms as specific as possible. For example, instead of just typing in "tsunamis," try "tsunami preparedness Oregon Coast." That should narrow the possibilities from thousands down to dozens.

Search for organizations involved in your subject. Does your featured artist belong to the National Watercolor Society or a sculptors' guild? Does his gallery have a website? Can you find reviews that have been published about his work?

Most published articles will mention organizations, websites, individuals and other sources. Often you can use a small portion of an article if it appears in an authoritative journal and cite the source, writing something like: According to a December 11, 2007 TIME Magazine article…

Your search will probably take more time than you expect, but it won't take nearly as long as it would if you had to go to the library and search for all of your information in person.

Most of what you need can be found on the Internet, but you may still wind up at the library for specific books or magazine articles.

Ask the reference librarian to help you find relevant brochures, books, databases and directories. These days, librarians are not just book people but electronic media experts.

If your library is like ours, it has its own website. You can prowl through its databases and check the library catalog from home. You can also reserve books that you want to check out from that library or from other libraries, so you can have them waiting for you when you get there. If you have access to a university library, you can find even more databases full of articles and information. Even if you are not a student or employee at the university, you can usually check out books or do research there for a modest fee.

While you're at the library, check Gale's *Encyclopedia of Associations* for organizations related to your story. The right organization can lead you to people who have exactly the information you need, plus photos, charts, statistics and more.

Back issues of newspapers can be a great source of information. The public library probably has some hidden away. The older issues will be on CD-Rom or on microfilm. You can usually look up the article and print out a copy for free or a few cents a page.

Sometimes it's best to go straight to the newspaper itself. The *New York Times* has an online index listing articles back to 1851. You can download copies of these articles for a small fee. Other papers may not be as organized, but it's worth checking. Most newspaper online archives only go back a few years, but that may be all you need.

Before they started their online archives, newspapers saved their stories on paper in their own libraries, often called morgues. Many dailies have a staff librarian who will look up your subject and send you clippings by mail, e-mail or fax. There may be a fee for this service, but reading the stories that other people have written on the subject can save you a lot of work.

Some smaller papers have well-organized clip files they will let you look through. At other papers, you could wind up in the conference room going page by page through back issues to find stories on your subject. This is time-consuming, but you're bound to find more story ideas while you're looking.

Primary Sources

What you find on the Internet and at the library are called *secondary sources*, information that has already been published. These are important for background material. But the best sources for newspaper articles are usually interviews. They often provide you the most up-date-information, fresh information nobody else has. Straight from the horse's mouth, so to speak. These are considered *primary sources*.

Even if you are an expert in your subject, it will make your article stronger if you collect material from other sources to back up your statements. Most people love to talk about their work and their lives. If you call and explain what you need, they will nearly always agree to an interview.

If you're doing a feature on a person, one primary source is obvious. You need to interview that person. We have all read celebrity pieces that are done without actually talking to the celebrity. The writer simply cobbles together quotes from various articles and perhaps a few interviews from people who know the celebrity. The story may read all right, but that method really isn't fair to the subject or the reader. Unless the person is dead or in a coma, try hard to talk to him or her.

I don't mean you shouldn't interview people who know your subject. These people can add another point of view and tell you things he might not say about himself.

For the tsunami story, you will want to interview the people preparing for the big wave. You might talk to folks at the Red Cross, especially if you can find someone who went overseas to help the victims of a previous tsunami. Can you locate someone who was vacationing or working there when it happened? How about someone local whose house or business would be right in the path of a tsunami if it hit your town? Are they worried? Have they done anything to prepare?

Make a list of people to interview. How do you find them? The first place to look is a reporter's best friend, the telephone book. The source may be listed, and voilà, there's the number. If you need a number outside your local calling area, you could look through the out-of-town phone books at the library. But you don't even have to leave home. Both yellow pages and white pages are online. Often a Google search will turn up an expert's website with contact information.

In the case of the artist, perhaps you can ask the gallery manager, who will probably be glad to give you the artist's number and might even set up the interview for you. After all, it's free publicity.

For the tsunami story, sources can be located through previous articles, through organizations, or again, the telephone book. Government agencies are easy to find, but it might take you some time wading through "press 1, press 2, press 3, please hold" to connect with the right person. The Red Cross and other help organizations can also put you in touch with possible sources.

Many agencies have public relations people whose job is to talk to the press. They can be a great help, as long as you are clear about the story you are doing and don't let them dictate what to write. They can set up interviews and shower you with booklets, brochures, clippings and website addresses. In some cases, they are the only way to get to your sources. Just remember that they are paid to say positive things about the organization or its people and products.

These days, most people have e-mail addresses. If you are shy, live far away or have limited time for telephone calls, you can send an e-mail requesting an interview. You can even send your questions, especially if you're just looking for a brief quote or a specific piece of information.

Ask everyone you talk to if they have anything in writing they can send you, and ask them who else might be good to interview. Perhaps the guy you talk to at the Red Cross can offer only a tiny piece of the tsunami story, but he knows someone else who is deeply involved in it. He can also alert his friend that you're going to call, so that when you do call, he already knows who you are and what you want.

Universities are fertile sources for interview subjects. Call the public relations or communications office to make connections. Several private organizations will also link reporters with experts in various fields. Online try Profnet.Prnewswire.com and Experts.com.

Keep your eyes and ears open for anything that might be related to what you are writing. Always keep your questions in mind. It's like a scavenger hunt. Will this newspaper article or this person help me answer these questions? Tell your friends, family and coworkers what you're looking for. If they don't have the answers themselves, they might be able to give you the name of a great source, and even provide a personal introduction.

You won't use every piece of information you collect, and that's fine. You should always know more than you put on the page. Gregg Levoy, author of *This Business of Writing*, says, "If you do it right, you will inevitably end up using only a fraction of the research material you generate. And once you begin to write, you must use the eye of a sculptor to help you carve away what you don't want and reveal the true story beneath it."

So Many Notes!

If your handwriting is terrible, like mine, type up everything as soon as you get home, while the information is still fresh in your mind. Otherwise, you could find yourself staring at a scribble trying to figure out what you wrote down.

It really doesn't matter how you organize your research as long as you can find and understand what you have gathered and know exactly where it came from. You could go into an elaborate system of file cards, folders or colored magic markers or set up a database on your computer. That's fine, if you have time, but you can also just jot a few key words in the margins of your notes.

Some cautions:

> • Keep track of the source of every piece of information you use in your story. You will want to be able to access it again if the editor has questions, and you may need to be able to prove where you got the information. It is helpful—and required by some publications—to make a list of the people you interview, with names, addresses, telephone numbers, and e-mail addresses, along with lists of written material and other sources you use. Sometimes the editor will ask for a list. Even if she doesn't, you'll find it handy if you need

to contact any of the sources or want to do a future article on a related subject.

Don't throw this information away for at least a year after the story is published. This is your protection against editors, sources, and readers who dispute what you say.

• Save all of your research, either on your computer or printed out on paper. Don't toss anything. If you don't need it for this story, you might use it for a spinoff later.

• Don't believe everything you read or everything people tell you. Be suspicious of anything that sounds like advertising or propaganda. Look for at least two sources that say the same thing for any controversial information. One story I wrote involved a group that claimed their festival was the "biggest Portuguese feast in the world." Two weeks after I attended that feast, I found another group that claimed their festival was even bigger. For another story, I wrote that a new commuter airline would be the first ever to fly out of our local airport. A reader let me know that another airline had served our town back in the 1950s, long before I moved here. Be leery of anyone who says he has the biggest, the only, the first, the best, etc. Assume there's another one out there somewhere unless you can verify that what they say is true.

• Don't let your own personal biases keep you from seeing, hearing and reporting the facts.

• Don't plagiarize. Don't copy things verbatim from written materials without giving proper credit in the articles. If you use more than a few lines you must get permission from the copyright owner. If you're writing for a newspaper, you probably won't have time to do that, so recast the material in your own words. You can't copyright ideas or information, only the way in which they are expressed.

Without evidence, your stories will be like the legal case with nothing to back it up. Your sentences may be smooth, your spelling perfect, your paragraphs well-formed and logical, but if you have no details, no facts to support your generalities, your writing will seem empty, as if it is missing something important—which it is.

Exercise

- Plan the research for an article for one of the queries you wrote for the last chapter or for an article on another subject. List questions you will need to answer and sources you will use. If you have time, or if you already have an assignment, start your research and try to set up an interview or two.

Chapter 6

Conducting Effective Interviews

An interview is a conversation. But unlike a normal conversation, one person is asking questions, and the other is answering, knowing that whatever he says could wind up in print. An interview is purposely a one-sided conversation. You need to know about the other person or what he knows, but he does not need to know about you. Indeed, to the interviewee, we are not an individual; we are the newspaper we write for.

In some ways, an interview is like a performance. You sometimes have only one shot at asking your questions, and the interviewee has only one shot at answering them. If you don't get what you need, you may find a hole in your notes that is difficult to fill. If the interviewee forgets to tell you something, discloses something he wanted to keep private, or is not his usual self because he's sick, stressed or just having a bad day, he may regret the interview and the subsequent story. Chances are you're both nervous. But actors and musicians say a little stage fright makes for a better performance.

An interview is somewhat like a business meeting in that the writer comes armed with questions—an agenda—and when the questions are answered or the scheduled time has expired, the meeting is over. You, the writer, generally come dressed up and trying to look and sound professional. Even if you meet over a meal, it is not the same as eating with friends. This is a business lunch.

An interview is a conversation unlike any other. As Marcia Yudkin, author of *Freelance Writing for Magazines and Newspapers*, writes, "Interviewing demands almost as much adeptness and concentration as tightrope walking."

Let's look at how to make it work.

Setting up the Interview

If you can interview someone in person, do it. That allows you to catch them in their natural habitat, which will help you to set the scene in your story. It also usually means you can spend more time with them. If there is something to see, whether it's how the artist does his work or what buildings will be wiped out by the tsunami, it is better to see it while you are hearing about it.

If you live too far away or the interviewee doesn't have time, you can schedule a telephone interview or ask your questions by e-mail. Many people who won't agree to a face-to-face interview for one reason or another will agree to an e-mail interview. E-mail is also a great way to ask follow-up questions after the initial interview.

Set up the interview as soon as you get the assignment. Most people seem to need at least a week's notice to fit an interview into their schedule. They may be traveling, home with the flu, or so busy that every minute is already planned for the next week or two. You might also have to play phone tag trying to reach them. So start calling as soon as possible. If they don't call back in twenty-four hours, call again. All too often, when I call a second or third time, the source says he has been meaning to call. If you have only a few days or a week to do the article, tell them. Sometimes if you give them a deadline, space magically appears in their schedule.

Cold-calling a source can be pretty daunting. I still get tongue-tied on these calls. But know that you'll probably get their voice mail the first go-round, and that most people are glad to help you. It might help at first to write down what you're going to say. Some interviewers script every word, others jot down the points they want to mention, and others just have faith that the words will come when they need them.

When you call, tell the source right away who you are, what you are writing about and for whom you are writing it. Never pretend to be someone else or deny that you're writing an article. If you don't have a firm assignment yet, you can still say that you're working on an article that you hope to publish in a particular newspaper. Tell them that you would like to schedule an interview. If they resist, be polite but persistent. Don't get into an argument with them. Everyone has the right to say no to an interview, and you might have to accept that as your answer. However, if you courteously urge them to help you get all sides of an issue, they may yield after a bit.

Sometimes subjects will ask you to shoot your questions at them then and there. If you're ready, go ahead, especially if you suspect you won't ever have the chance again. However, if you are not prepared or if you would rather meet in person, tell them you would prefer to set up an appointment when you can both devote some time to it. It is better to do your secondary research first so that you can ask intelligent questions without wasting time on the kinds of things you ought to already know. Setting up an interview in the future also gives the subject time to think about what he'll say and to gather some information.

Even if you're going to do the interview on the telephone, you can set up a specific time to call. That way they can be sure to be available, with someone else answering other calls and with no pressure to speak quickly so they can get to the next thing on their agenda. If you are working from home, this gives you a chance to put the dog out, turn the music off, and set up the tape or digital recorder. Unless your sources insist otherwise, you will call them, absorbing any long-distance charges.

Interviews can take place at a person's home or office or where they are involved in a project. These are the best because they are usually quiet and add atmosphere to the story. Unless it's the only way to find time, avoid breakfast, lunch or dinner interviews. First of all, you're going to pay for it and probably won't be reimbursed. Second, restaurants are often noisy and not particularly private. Third, it's nearly impossible to juggle a fork and a pen at the same time. Every time you ask a question, the subject will have his mouth full; every time he says something good, you'll be about to take a bite, so you never actually get to eat. It's a sure path to indigestion. If you are recording it, all you might get is clinking dishes and background music. If the source insists on meeting over a meal, go ahead, but suggest a relatively quiet location. Perhaps you could start in the office, getting the main information there, then move on to lunch.

Meeting for coffee or a drink isn't so bad because your hands are free. In mid-afternoon, most restaurants, bars or hotel lobbies are pretty quiet. If you're drinking alcohol, know your limits. If you get silly after one drink, nurse that one through the whole interview or order something nonalcoholic. Likewise, if your source gets soused, the interview could turn out badly.

For some stories, where all you need are straight facts and where links to websites would be helpful, e-mail interviews are great. Round-ups, where you are essentially putting together a glorified list, a survey, or a collection of quotes, are a perfect example. But e-mail isn't always the best course. If you get an agreement to an e-mail interview ahead of time most people will honor their agreement but you can never be certain when, or if, they will respond. If you let them know when your deadline is, you are more likely to get a quick response.

And, of course, with e-mail, you can't get any atmosphere or visual cues, nor can you give or receive spontaneous responses to what is said. On the other hand, e-mail allows you to question people you might otherwise miss because they are too busy or worried about being put on the spot with questions they don't want to answer or don't know how to answer. E-mail is wonderful because it allows you to interview people all over the world at any hour of the day, and to work in your pajamas. E-mail interviews also provide a written record of the conversation, which can be helpful for both of you.

Take care in writing your e-mail questions. You won't be there in person to clarify or to ask follow-up questions. Try to keep your list of questions as short as possible and ask if you may send a follow-up list if necessary.

Don't Go Unprepared

Just as you would not wing it for a stage performance or a business meeting, you should not wing it with an interview. It is all too likely that you will run out of questions after fifteen minutes, that you won't get the information you need, or that you'll be so disorganized the source will think you're an idiot. Preparation is essential.

Study

Read everything you can about the subject before you get there. Nothing irritates sources more than questions for which any professional reporter ought to already know the answers. Don't come in, look around and say, "Well, what do you do here?" If you don't know, you're not ready. In fact, while you're setting up the interview, it doesn't hurt to ask if there's any background material they can send you or a website you can look up on the Internet.

Confirm the Interview

People, being human, sometimes forget about your interview. Sometimes they need to change the time or the location, but they have lost the note with your telephone number on it.

If it has been more than a couple of days since you set up the interview, call or e-mail to make sure the person is still expecting you. This is a good time to ask for directions if you need them.

Allow Plenty of Time to Get There

Surely I'm not the only one who gets lost in unfamiliar places. Give yourself twice the time you think you will need to get there. If you arrive with time to spare, use the restroom, scope out the location, study your questions or relax for a few minutes. If you get lost, it will give you extra time to find your way. If you get hopelessly lost, call from a cell phone or a pay phone to tell them your situation and ask them how to get there. Likewise, if for some reason you can't make it to the interview—heaven forbid—or if you know you're going to be late, always call.

Dress the Part

Not every interview requires dress-up attire, but it is good to fit in with the folks you're interviewing. If you are going to a downtown corporate office or a government building to interview people in suits and ties, you too should be wearing a suit and tie if you're a man or a nice dress, skirt suit or pantsuit if you're a woman. If you're going into the wilderness to talk with a park ranger, to the docks to do a boating story or to a farm to talk about cows, clean casual clothes are fine; in fact this is wiser than dressing up. High heels in the cow pasture would be ridiculous, but so would tennis shoes in the board room. Be yourself, but be aware that first impressions count.

Take Your Tools

Invest in a briefcase, file bag, big purse or something else that looks nice and can hold everything you need. What goes in it?

• **Notebook.** Size and shape depends on your personal preference. Some writers swear by those little white reporter notebooks that fit in your pocket. I like steno pads, which are a little bigger. Others write only on 8-inch by 10-inch yellow pads. Your choice should be big enough for you to write legibly and it ought to look professional. Your son's Sesame Street tablet with the dotted lines won't do. Expect to fill lots of pages if the interview goes well.

• **Pens.** Bring at least two. The last thing you need is to run out of ink in the middle of an interview and have to beg a source to loan you a pen.

• **A tape or digital recorder.** This is not essential. In fact, for some brief interviews, it's more trouble than it's worth, but if you are going into any depth or, as happens fairly often, you will be walking as you talk, it is wonderful to have the machine getting all those quotes that you can't possibly write down. It is also protection in case the source later says, "I didn't say that."

The recorder allows you to give yourself more freely to the conversation, looking the person in the eye and responding to what he says rather than struggling to write down what he just said and coming up with the next question at the same time. Most people speak at roughly 130 words per minute, faster when they're excited.

Most of us can't even type that quickly. Many writers take notes as well as use a recorder. This works as a backup in the event the recording fails and allows them to jot notes to themselves including follow-up questions to ask before the interview concludes.

The recorder does not need to be fancy or expensive, just dependable. Always bring an extra tape or media card and fresh batteries, and always test it at home, in the car, or in the restroom before you go into the interview. While you're testing, you can record the name of the person, the date and what story the interview is for.

• **A list of questions.** This will echo the questions you wrote in planning your research, with additional questions aimed at this particular source. You don't need to write them out in detail, just a few words to trigger your memory. It may happen that you don't need to use the questions, that the interview will flow naturally from one topic to another, but if it stalls or if you are afraid you'll forget to ask something important, it's comforting to have the questions there.

• **Business cards.** These days everyone has a card, and they will expect you to have one, too. It is evidence that you are a professional. Your card doesn't have to be elaborate. Plain black ink on white card stock is fine. You can buy a thousand cards at many places for less than thirty dollars. You can also buy blank cards at the office supply store and print your own, using software you probably have on your computer. Stick to the basics: name, address, e-mail address, phone

number and a line or two that says you're a freelance
writer.

A Few Tips

Typically you ask a question, the source speaks, you write down
what he says, and you go on to another question. It's not easy to juggle
these tasks all at once, especially if the person speaks quickly, but never
ask him or her to slow down. It calls attention to the fact that you are
recording, which makes people self-conscious. Also, have your notebook out and visible from the start. Some people panic when you
suddenly reveal your notebook. Over time, you will develop your own
shorthand way of note-taking, putting down key words, using abbreviations and symbols, such as %, <, >, w/o, etc., and you will find it
easier to keep up.

Don't trust your tape or digital recorder. Always take notes, too.
The one time you don't will be the one time your recorder doesn't
work. Turn the machine on quietly without fanfare and let it run. Assure the person you are interviewing that you are using the recording
only to ensure accuracy and will not share it with anyone else. Most
people don't mind, but if the source objects to recording, don't argue.
Just turn it off and make do with your notes. Don't ever try to hide the
recorder. It's unethical and illegal.

Doing the Interview

You arrive, shake hands and are escorted into a house, office,
conference room, restaurant booth or other location. Perhaps at this
point, the interviewee surprises you with one or more extra people
you didn't expect, perhaps a coworker, spouse, or public relations
person. Greet them cordially, and include them in the conversation,
especially if they can help with your story. One-on-one is easier, but
don't raise a fuss if your source has invited other people to make him
feel more comfortable.

Sometimes you may also have to deal with kids and pets. Try to
set it up so you have a quiet, uninterrupted situation, but if you can't

get out of it, smile indulgently at the children and pet the dog. If you are allergic to dogs, cats, birds or whatever, say so. It's hard to conduct an interview with your nose running, your eyes burning or welts breaking out all over your body.

Interviewees may offer you coffee, tea, soft drinks, and even snacks. Be sensitive as to whether they're just being polite or have gone to a lot of trouble to prepare something for you. If they baked you a cake, try a little, even if you never eat sweets. If they insist you have something and you really don't want anything, a glass of water is easy and gets the obligation out of the way. In other words, use your best manners.

Begin with a few minutes of small talk to break the ice. The weather, the dog you just met in the front yard, the art on the walls, and the drive over are all fodder for a little human-to-human conversation. But don't spend too long on it; you are here for a purpose. In some cases, the person will have only a set time to give you, and you want to make sure you use every minute wisely. Sometimes once the interview gets rolling, the time limit will disappear, but other times, people coming for the next meeting will arrive early or the interviewee will announce that he's out of time, get up and leave you talking to yourself, so do watch the clock.

The interviewee may ask you to tell him again why you're there. He might want to know about the newspaper you're writing for and what this story is all about. Explain it as clearly as you can, then get down to your questions. Get his full name and the correct spelling of it right away. Don't assume that John is J-O-H-N. It might be J-O-N or J-E-A-N or something else. Smith may actually be S-M-Y-T-H-E. If needed, also ask his age, job title and other pertinent information that is easy to get now but a pain to track down later. Ask for a business card or, if they are on a counter or desk, snag one.

Move into background questions and ease toward the heart of your subject. Don't be afraid to enter controversial territory. Ask questions that begin, "Is it true that…?" or "One of your competitors says that…."

You might save the most controversial questions until late in the interview, just in case the person decides to end the interview at that point. Most people are glad for a chance to tell their side of the story.

If the person announces that the interview is over, you may already have most of the information you need. Of course controversial questions are often the most important so don't wait so long to pop them that you run out of time.

Be conscious that it may seem you are being inordinately nosy, that the interviewee may be anxious about being interviewed, and that the subject matter may be sensitive or personal to him when it may not seem so to you. Try to be patient and encouraging, no matter how weird, rude or ignorant the person might appear to you. If you don't feel any rapport, fake it. This is an interview, not an interrogation. If you handle it right, the person will be flattered and eager to talk.

Gregg Levoy writes: "Most people, I believe, despite their protestations, want to be revealed or, more to the point, recognized. And interviewing, I think, is largely the ability to make people feel safe enough to be themselves in your presence. If they trust you, and if you are utterly attentive, your problem will not be getting them to open up but quite the opposite."

Ask about anything you don't understand. If he rattles off an acronym, ask what it stands for. It's better to admit your lack of knowledge now than try to make sense of it later. Don't guess, and don't take anything for granted. Besides, they'll know if you're bluffing. Years ago, I was doing a story on wood stoves. As we wandered among the various models, I asked so many stupid questions that the shop owner finally stopped and glared at me. "You don't know anything about this stuff, do you?" No, I didn't. I hadn't done my homework, but even if you have prepared as well as you can, it's perfectly all right to ask for basic information or clarifications rather than muddle through.

Share a little of yourself. Sometimes it encourages others to talk if you tell them about yourself, but don't go overboard. You are there to find out about them, to find out what their story is, what they think, what they do. You already know all about yourself, and this is a professional meeting, not the beginning of a friendship. Sometimes interviews do lead to friendships, but more often if you pass each other on the street six months from now, neither of you will remember who the other person is.

Encourage him to tell stories. Questions such as

- What was the best or the worst time of your life?
- What did you want to be when you were growing up?
- How did you feel when you lost the race? or
- What do you still want to accomplish before you die?

These types of questions often will lead to great anecdotes.

Ask open-ended questions that can't be answered with a yes or no. Don't ask, "How long have you been doing this?" Say, "Tell me how you got started…." Don't ask, "Do you have any hobbies?" Ask, "What do you do in your spare time?" Ask questions such as "What do you mean?" "How?" "Why?" or "What happened next?"

If a question is not answered, try restating it in another way. You might have to go on with the interview and return to the question a few minutes later.

If an answer is fuzzy, try parroting it back, saying something like, "So what you're saying is…." If there seems to be more that could be said, ask a follow-up question, such as "Why do you say that?"

Never be afraid to ask for more details. If you are doing a story on a remodeled house, it's fine to ask how they got that speckled paint on the walls or what that gadget in the kitchen is called. You can even ask how much the remodel cost. They might refuse to answer, but it's worth a try.

Listen

Don't be so busy framing your next question that you forget to listen to what the person is saying. Don't push for the answers you want; listen to the answers you get. If it changes your story, so be it.

The interviewee should do most of the talking. In some interviews, all you have to do is ask the first question and the person talks for an hour, giving you everything you need to know and more. Other people need you to guide them and encourage them. Be an active listener, nodding, saying, "Yes," "Uh-huh," "That's amazing," "What happened then?" and so on. Your interest will draw them out and keep them talking. Let there be silence between statements and allow the other person to be the first to break that silence.

A source may head off on a tangent that has nothing to do with your story. It is your job to gently steer him back to the subject. However, if something unexpected but interesting comes up, let him talk. Likewise, if you think of a question that you hadn't thought of before, go ahead and ask it.

If you don't believe something the interviewee says, politely ask him to clarify or repeat it. If he stands by it, verify the questionable material via other sources after the interview. Be especially wary of words and phrases like *the only, the best, the first, always* and *never.* Is this guy really the first marathoner to run from Portland, Oregon, to Portland, Maine? Check it out later.

Off the Record

People who are interviewed a lot will sometimes declare that what they are about to tell you is off the record. If you accept that, you are bound to honor their request. I usually put my pen down and turn off the tape recorder at that point. Not recording what they say doesn't mean that you don't hear it, that it doesn't go into your mind and your thoughts, but you cannot use that material or quote what the person says. Ever. Anywhere. If you would rather not hear what you can't write, say so.

If what is said while off the record is really wonderful stuff, try convincing the person to let you use it or at least include it without his name, but tread carefully here. Also, don't allow anyone you interview to change something to off the record hours or days after the fact. He knows you're a writer. He said it, and he can't take it back later.

Mannerisms

Watch their body language. Most of what you take home will be what the sources said, but also observe their posture, their gestures, their wardrobe, how they treat other people who come around while you're there. Sharing what your subject looked like and how he acted will convince the reader that you interviewed a live human being, not just a talking machine.

Ending It

Gradually you will run out of time or questions or both. Ask if there's anything else you failed to cover that they want to say. Then wind down the discussion by saying something like, "I think you have answered all my questions" or "I really appreciate your taking the time to talk to me." But don't put your notebook away yet. Some of the best quotes come after the official part of the interview is over. Everyone relaxes, and sometimes sources say fascinating things.

When it really is over, ask if you can call with any questions that come up later—and get a direct telephone number or e-mail address. Also ask if there are other people they would recommend that you talk to. If for some reason, you feel as if you haven't really gotten the story yet or you need to meet again, perhaps in another location, it's all right to ask for another meeting.

For some articles, the real story comes not from questions and answers but from watching the person in action or even getting into

Can I See It Before It Runs?

What if they want to see the story before you run it? About one-third of the people I interview ask to see a copy of the story before it goes to press. Say no. Most newspapers have a policy against letting sources see stories in advance. That is not because the press is trying to trick anyone or sneak anything past them but because of the natural tendency of people to want to completely rewrite the story, change their quotes and otherwise drive the editor crazy. Do offer to confirm any facts that you or they might have doubts about. You can also offer to read, fax, or e-mail any specific quotes that you are using from the person, but tell him it's against company policy to let sources see the story before publication. Which company? Both the newspaper and your freelance writing company of one.

the action yourself. If the bird expert invites you to go bird-watching with him, you might have to get up early in the morning, but you could find the heart of your story as you peer through your binoculars looking for that yellow-bellied sapsucker.

Telephone Interviews

Interviews over the telephone work pretty much the same as in-person interviews, except that you don't have to dress up and you don't get visual cues or the same sense of atmosphere. Go there in person if you can, but if you can't, the phone is fine. In fact, sometimes people actually say more over the telephone, especially if you sound friendly and nonthreatening. Smile when you talk, speak slowly and clearly, and hide any frustration or anger that you may feel. You still want to proceed with a list of questions, have an extra pen handy and keep your professional attitude intact. Take the baby to the babysitter's and put the dog out. Tell anyone else in the house that you are doing an interview and should not be disturbed. You might close the door to the room you are in and hang a sign that says something like: Interviewing. Please don't disturb.

You can record from the telephone. Some telephones come with built-in recording devices. If yours doesn't have one, electronics stores sell inexpensive adapters that will link your recorder to the telephone. In most places it is required by law that you tell the other person you are recording him. Assure him this is for accuracy, that no one else will hear the recording. Now that I'm in the bifocal years, I joke about not being as fast or as sharp as I used to be, and people don't mind.

As in person-to-person interviews it is a good idea to take handwritten notes, too.

After the Interview

As soon as you are somewhere private, check your recorder to make sure it worked properly. If it didn't, you'll need to add to any notes you took, writing down everything you can possibly remember before you forget it. If it worked—and it usually does—put the recording somewhere safe where it can't be accidentally recorded over, melted in the sun, sat on, or lost before you have time to transcribe it.

Go over your notes, filling in the blanks, clearing up words you can't read, and writing down your observations about the place, the way the person looked, things you heard, smelled or sensed while you were there. Number each page and write down the name of the source so that if your pages get separated later you can figure out what you have.

Relax

Then go home and type out your notes, transcribing the recording if you have one, adding your personal observations, putting it all into sensible sentences. You may want to organize your notes by topic and sub-topic—or you can type them as they come and mark them up later with different-colored felt pens or Post-It notes.

After the article is published, write a brief thank you note to your main sources. Enclose a copy of the article or let them know where they can find a copy at a newsstand or online. You may want to seek a source's help again for future stories, so be nice. He'll remember the little acts of kindness.

Moving toward the Article

Depending on the subject of your article, the requirements of the newspaper and other factors, you may do one interview or a dozen. You will accumulate a lot of notes, articles, brochures and other material. Keep it all, along with your list of questions. That list will guide you when you write your article.

How do you know you have enough information? When you find that you're getting the same answers for the third or fourth time, when you realize that you know more than most people know about the subject, when you just can't think of anything else to ask, you're probably ready. If you're itching to write the story, then it's definitely time to starting putting words together.

With practice, you will get good at interviewing and the butterflies that dance in your stomach now will go away. In fact, interviews will become fun. After all, you get to meet interesting people and sample different worlds that most people never experience.

Exercise

• Interview someone. If you have an article underway, set up and conduct an interview. If you are not ready to do this for an actual article, try interviewing a relative or a friend. For example, sit down with your grandfather or your uncle and ask him about his childhood. How did he meet his wife? What was it like moving here from another state or another country? How were things different in his younger days? If he could relive any event in his life, what would it be?

Or you could ask a friend to tell you about his job. What does he do? How would he describe a typical day? What does he like best about his work? What are his plans for the future? Would he mind if you tagged along and took notes for a few hours?

You might also visit a senior center or nursing home and ask the residents about their lives. Take notes just as if you were going to write an article. Who knows? Your practice interview might lead to a real story.

Chapter 7

Writing the Newspaper Article

$\mathbf{W}$riting the newspaper article is a blend of craft and artistry. We have all heard the saying "Just the facts, ma'am," but if all we provided were facts, our stories would be so dull that no one would want to read them. We need to hook the readers with an opening they can't resist, then keep them reading all the way to the end.

Just as you must consider the audience for your article ideas, you also need to consider the audience when writing the article. Are they young, old or a mixture of all ages? Are they college-educated or barely literate? Do they live in the city or the country? Are they rich, poor, or somewhere in between? Are they likely to know anything about your topic, or will they need to have everything explained?

I have often heard that newspapers are written for readers at an eighth-grade level. I don't believe that's universally true, but it is generally a less sophisticated type of writing than you will find in academic journals or in magazines like *The New Yorker*. There are exceptions, such as the *Wall Street Journal*, but mostly we're writing for the masses, for our families, our friends, doctors, lawyers, construction workers, and the teenager who bags our groceries.

It is important not to "write down" to your readers; to do so is likely to come across as condescending. Still, we cannot assume that our readers know things most people would not know and, as in any writing, clarity is king. We should also be aware that people read newspapers in a hurry. While they might linger over a book and even take the time to look up an unfamiliar word or reread a confusing passage, when reading the newspaper, they are more likely to move on to the next story or toss the paper into the recycle bin if anything slows them down.

Newspaper writing should flow naturally. We should write like we speak—only better. We take out the *ums* and the *uhs*, the bad grammar, the wasted words and the unsubstantiated allegations. We use more accurate, colorful language, in organized paragraphs and sentences that make sense. We are telling a story. Just because it's true doesn't mean we can't use some of the techniques of fiction, including dialogue, scenes, settings, even suspense. True stories are often more interesting than fictional ones.

Always keep in mind, the most important function of a newspaper article is to convey information.

Choices

You don't have to use every bit of information or every quote you gather. Most newspaper articles are short, so you won't have room for everything.

Writing an article entails a series of choices: What shall I write about? Whom shall I interview? What information will I put in my story and what will I leave out?

It is important to recognize that you control what is being communicated to the reader. Although it is often criticized for not doing it well enough, a free press is meant to transmit information without bias. Statistics and statements can be twisted to make something appear different than it is. Politicians do this all the time; it's called *spin*.

Our job as journalists is to present the information as clearly and accurately as possible and let the readers make up their own minds.

This means we have to be diligent in digging up the whole story, even if we'd rather not make an extra phone call or spend time checking a fact we're not sure of.

After you turn your story in, the editor's decisions about revisions, headlines, and placement in the paper will also affect what the reader gets out of the piece, but your job is to write well and truthfully.

Sage Advice

In *The Elements of Style*, a superb book every writer should read yearly, William Strunk, Jr. and E. B. White offer sage advice applicable to all the newspaper articles—and other types of writing—you undertake. Here's a sampling:

• *Use the active voice.* Many times this can be accomplished by replacing the verb *to be* in all its forms. Substitute
The soldiers suddenly appeared on the ridge.
for
The soldiers suddenly could be seen on the ridge.
• *Use definite, specific, concrete language.* To use Strunk and White's exact words: "Prefer the specific to the general, the definite to the vague, the concrete to the abstract."
• *Omit needless words.* This advice is even more appropriate today with readers' attention spans seemingly growing shorter by the year. Check every sentence you write and see if you can't recast it with fewer words.

If you don't have a copy of *The Elements of Style*, drop your plans for this afternoon and get to the bookstore.

Word Count

Most of the time, you will be assigned a specific number of words for your article. It will rarely feel like enough, but editors usually have a specific number of column inches into which the stories must fit. Try to come within 10 percent of the specified length. On occasion this may mean adding to the story, but most likely, you will need to cut. Cutting is a difficult thing to do, but there are always wordy sentences that can be put on a diet and information you can summarize or skip. Never pad an article with extra words or irrelevant information. If need be, do more research so you'll have more to write about.

Most word-processing programs have a word count function, usually under the tools menu.

Point of View

Most newspaper articles are written in the third person, which means you write about people using *he, she* or *they. He* did this, *she* did that. In standard newspaper fare you don't refer to yourself, so you don't use the pronoun *I* which would be writing in the first person. You also don't usually use the second person, where you address the reader as *you* (as I did in this sentence).

The exceptions to this rule are columns and opinion pieces, in which you are expected to write in the first person, and how-to's, where it is permissible to address the reader as *you.* Look at the paper for which you are writing to see how it handles point of view and do likewise.

Tense

Most newspaper articles are written in past tense. This means you write about something as if it happened in the past, which it most likely did. Use *said* instead of *says, walked* instead of *walks,* etc.

Get Organized

You have a pile of notes and research materials, you know a lot about your subject, and you have the answers to the questions you set out to ask. You are ready to write your article.

Ideally, by the time you finish researching and interviewing, you will be so filled with your story that the words will just bubble out of their own accord. Don't worry about format or anything else at this point; just write, letting your words flow from one idea to the next. You can perfect it later.

However, if the words don't tumble onto the screen, if you are staring at the blank screen and don't know where to begin, you need a process.

First, go through your notes. Make a list of the different types of information you have and use key words to mark where you can find those topics in your notes. Your list will probably be very similar to your list of questions. Say you're writing about the people who take care of the whales at an aquarium. You have information about:

- The whales themselves–how big they are, where they came from, their individual needs or personality traits
- The caretakers and their backgrounds
- The whale caretakers' daily schedule
- What they feed the whales, how it's delivered and how often
- Other things they do with the whales
- Details about the birth of a baby whale at the aquarium last year
- Plans to expand the whale exhibit

Each of these topics will ultimately become one or more paragraphs of your story. Your list is your outline. You don't need to worry about roman numerals and *A*s and *B*s. No teacher is going to check your outline for perfect form. In fact, if calling it an outline makes you feel uncomfortable, call it a checklist.

Now that you know what you have, number the items on your list in the order you think they'll work best. All you have to do now is string them together like pearls on a necklace. The first trick is to find the biggest, most interesting pearl to get your story started.

Write First, Edit Later

On your first draft, don't worry too much about the details. Let it flow. If you are missing a piece of information, leave a series of *X*s or a question to yourself in brackets and come back to it later. If you don't know how to spell a word, do your best and figure it out on the next draft. If you're not sure the article is any good, write it anyway. A story often evolves into a new shape by the time you get to the end. Once you have something to work with, it will be much easier to adapt and revise your story.

If you get stuck, it's probably because you have written yourself into a corner or aren't sure where you're going yet. Try these tricks to break through writer's block:

- Experiment with several different openings.

There's nothing wrong with trying five or six different starts before you find one that leads you easily into the body of the article. Sometimes the goofiest idea, the one you throw down out of desperation, becomes the perfect lead for your story.

• Bite off small pieces. If you tell yourself you have to write the whole thing at once, it might be so overwhelming that it paralyzes you. If you promise yourself you're only going to write one page or one section, you can do that much. Once you're warmed up, you'll probably go on. If you just can't, put it off a day and do the next section tomorrow—unless you're right on deadline. In that case, go for a brisk walk, then come back and try my next suggestion.

• Shove your notes aside and write what you know, summarizing the quotes that stick in your mind. You'll be surprised at how often the story falls easily into place. Then you can go back and add and polish up the details.

• Set the timer. Tell yourself you're only going to write for a half hour. If you absolutely cannot think of anything, fine, but you can't do anything else during that thirty minutes, after which you will reward yourself with food, a walk, a TV show or whatever else makes you happy. Chances are you'll get bored and start typing. I'll bet you won't want to stop when the timer goes off.

Use Quotes

People like to eavesdrop. In writing, the quotes you include allow the reader to eavesdrop. Quotes make the story come alive in a way nothing else can.

Rule number one when quoting: Write it the way they said it. It's okay to correct minor grammatical errors, but in general you need to repeat exactly what your source said. If a person's quotes are too jumbled or awkward, paraphrase them. Attribute the thought to him but leave the quote marks off.

As in other types of writing, you need to start a separate paragraph for each change of speaker whom you quote. For example:

> "I've been living on this ranch my whole life. I don't know any other life," Jake Barnes said.
>
> "But we can adapt," his wife, Julie, said. "At least I hope we can."

Perhaps you have a quote within a quote. Use single quotation marks to indicate the second speaker being quoted.

Jake shook his head. "Remember what that banker said: 'There's no way I can give you a loan based on a ranch that's about to be buried under a thousand tons of asphalt.'"

Don't use quotes out of context just to make your story work better. A journalist's job is to write the truth, even when it's clumsy.

Use Attribution

Be wary of making statements without attributing a particular piece of information to a source. If you say the sun rises in the east and sets in the west, no one will challenge you, but anything you can't attest to yourself needs to be attributed. You can say the rug was a dirty blue if you were there and saw it, otherwise you need to attribute it to the person or source you learned it from. In this instance you would write something like: According to Margaret Smith, the rug was a dirty blue. Another way to attribute a statement is to quote the speaker: "It certainly was a filthy blue rug," Margaret Smith said.

The All-Important Lead

When you look at the newspaper, do you read every article? Of course not. None of us has time to spend on stories that don't grab our interest. The first paragraph, the lead (sometimes spelled lede), is the most important paragraph of your story. In a news story, as opposed to a feature story, one duty of the lead is to tell the reader what happened. An easy way to develop this paragraph is to think of what you would say to your spouse or your best friend if you had only a minute to tell him what the story is all about. You rush in, breathless, shouting, "A boat just ran aground at Lost Creek! That's the third one this month. Thank God nobody was hurt this time." By the end of the first sentence, you have their attention, and in three sentences you have given the essence of the story.

In a news lead, it is important to spill the most important facts immediately. Tell us who, what, where, when and why right away, then, in the following paragraphs give us additional details in descending order of importance. You'll recall this is the inverted pyramid we've talked about. Its original purpose was to enable editors to trim stories from the bottom without taking away any vital information. But it's also important to give the busy reader who might only have time to read the beginning of the story the gist of what happened in a few tightly packed lines. If he isn't interested, he can just go on to the next story.

For a feature story, you have more leeway. You definitely need to get to the point soon, preferably by the third paragraph, but you can start in many ways, as long as your first few sentences pique the reader's interest and draw him into the story. We discussed writing leads in Chapter 4 when we were looking at writing queries. To recap, a good lead can be composed of anything and the best leads are fresh and compelling.

Here are a few of the standards with an example to illustrate each:

- A startling statistic: "Last year, 10,000 junior high school boys brought knives to school despite increased security and the installation of metal detectors." Or "Think your grocery bill is outrageous? Whales eat 500 pounds of food a day."
- A scene: "Jake Barnes leaned against a bale of hay, bit off a wad of chewing tobacco, and stared out at the sun setting over the cow pasture. He ignored the

government officials standing by the road talking about running a freeway right through his ranch. "Ah, I've heard all that before," Jake said.

• A quote: "Until I adopted Charlie, I didn't think I ever wanted kids. One look at his big blue eyes changed everything."

• An anecdote: "Peter will never forget the day he caught his first fish…."

Follow Your Lead

The lead should set you on the path for the rest of your article. The statistic on kids and knives would probably lead to a paragraph introducing the main topic, which is how school security programs have failed. The ranch scene might move into a paragraph about how this time it was really happening and the new freeway would disrupt the lives of Jake and others like him. The adoption quote could lead into a story on unusual adoptions or a trend toward older adoptive parents. The fishing story might segue into a feature on Peter's work as a commercial fisherman or his crusade to save his favorite fishing spot.

Your second or third paragraph, right after your lead, is a lot like the second paragraph of your query. In newspaper lingo, it is sometimes called the *nut graf*, because it sums everything up in a nutshell. This paragraph grounds the reader by explaining what's going on: Now that I have your attention, here's what I want to talk about. It could also be compared to the topic or thesis paragraph of an essay.

It is conventional wisdom that you should use a quote high up in every story. As you are interviewing, and, after the interview, as you go over the quotes you captured, look for a strong statement to use as this opening quote. The best ones are those which work to set the scene: "The softball players were dancing with joy" or display an emotion: "I feel like my brother has been ripped from my arms." Putting your first quote high up in the article helps hook the reader into reading the rest of it.

Make It Flow

Your story needs to move quickly. Picture the reader on a coffee break or waiting for a bus with very little time. Magazines offer more space for leisurely beginnings, and books offer even more, but with newspapers, you have to keep moving right from the start, and every paragraph should advance the story. If the person laying out the newspaper jumps your story to another page, you want the reader to feel compelled to turn to the page where the story continues.

With any luck, once you have written the lead and the nut graf, the story will flow from one point to another, using the topics in your outline, the ones you marked in your notes, until you have covered each topic.

It is up to you to make the connections for the reader from topic A to topic B within your story. Use connecting words and phrases such as *meanwhile, at the same time, although, however, in spite of,* etc.

A device that often works to help you see if the flow from concept to concept proceeds logically is to insert subheads when you make a transition to a new concept. Subheads also assist the reader. You don't want the reader to stop reading, thinking, "Hey, how did we get from whale food to *that*?" If the newspaper you're writing for doesn't use subheads, just strip them out before you send in the manuscript.

> ## Why Should the Reader Care?
>
> "Stories need to establish quickly–in the first few lines–why they are interesting and worth the read. Always ask why readers would care about the story, and answer as you write," note the *Christian Science Monitor* guidelines.

Circle Back

At the end of the story, it's good to complete the circle by harking back to what you said in the beginning–the quote, the scene, the statistic, your thesis statement. You might summarize the main points of the article or succinctly answer a question you posed at the beginning of the piece. This may also be the place you call for the reader to take action, whether it's making plans to visit the place in your travel article, calling the reader's congressman to demand he vote one way or another on the subject in your opinion piece, or getting started on that how-to project.

Depending on the type of article you're writing, you may want to end with websites to visit to find more information on the subject, contact information for making hotel reservations, or other types of helpful material. Check the newspaper to see how they format this information, then plug in the names, phone numbers, and e-mail addresses or websites.

Newspaper Style

Most newspapers use the *Associated Press Stylebook* to answer tricky questions about capitalization, hyphenation, dates, times, addresses, titles, brand names and other matters. It is an amazingly useful book and will answer all kinds of questions for you. Here are a few sample entries:

QE2: acceptable on second reference for the ocean liner Queen Elizabeth 2. (But use a roman numeral for the monarch: *Queen Elizabeth II*)

mid-: no hyphen unless a capitalized word follows:

mid-America	midsemester
mid-Atlantic	midterm

But use a hyphen when *mid-* precedes a figure: *mid-30s*.

smokejumper: one word, lowercase, for the firefighter who gets to fires by aircraft and parachute.

Some papers have their own style sheet which basically augments the *AP Stylebook*. Ask your editor if his paper has one. Adhering to proper style will please editors because you will be saving them lots of time putting your work into the correct style. Saving editors time is a great way to get the next assignment.

Use Short Paragraphs

Looking at a newspaper page, you can see that the stories are set up in columns, usually five or six to a broadsheet (full-size) page, three or four to a tabloid-size page. When forced into that format, a single sentence can take up several lines and a paragraph can go on forever. Therefore, newspaper articles are generally written in shorter paragraphs than other types of writing. A good rule of thumb is that if you've gotten to the fourth line on your page or computer screen, it's time to think about ending that paragraph and moving on to another.

Vary Sentence Length

Reading paragraph after paragraph of sentences of equal length gets monotonous. Too many long sentences at once tends to tire the reader. Many short sentences together creates an almost frenzied feeling. The best writers vary their sentence length, providing the reader with a pleasing cadence.

Use Active Verbs

Active verbs are more engaging than passive verbs and generally take up less space. Instead of "The whale *was fed* a bucket of raw anchovies every morning" write, "The whale *devoured* a bucket of raw anchovies every morning."

Be Specific

Don't write *flowers.* Write *roses.* Don't say he ate a *fish dinner.* Say he dined on *broiled halibut.* Instead of *several,* give us a specific number. If you can name a street or a neighborhood instead of just the city, that makes the story more alive to us.

Delete empty modifiers such as *really, truly, genuinely,* and *very.* Remove unneeded phrases such as "at this point in time" (why not simply write "now"?) or "it goes without saying" (so don't). Shorten wordy sentences. Instead of writing, "He is the type of man who is never afraid," write, "He is never afraid" or, even better, "Nothing scares him."

In all types of writing, including newspaper articles, strive to make every word count.

Include Sensory Details

Tell us how it looked, felt, smelled, and sounded. Take us beyond mere quotes and facts so that we not only read the story but experience it.

Sidebars

If a chunk of good material doesn't fit into the main story, think about writing a sidebar. A sidebar is basically a box that contains a shorter accompanying article or extra information. It could be a resource list, an anecdote, a brief biography or a collection of quotes. Usually these are under 300 words. Let the editor know if you'll be supplying a sidebar so he can allow space for it. Editors usually welcome sidebars because they help dress up the page, and readers like them as a quick source of information.

Formatting Your Manuscript

Hard Copy

As with the query letter, no editor will obsess over whether your manuscript's margins are one inch or an inch and a half, but following a standard manuscript format will make you appear as the professional you are. See "Standard Manuscript Format" on page 169, at the back of this book, for instructions on what a standard format looks like.

E-mail Manuscript Format

Today, most editors will want you to e-mail your material to them. If you send your text in the body of an e-mail, much of your formatting may disappear. Therefore your name, address, phone number, word count, etc., should all be flush left. Instead of indenting your paragraphs, put an extra space between them—unless the editor tells you otherwise. You won't need page numbers.

Be careful of using italics, quote marks, and boldfacing. In an e-mail, they are likely to either disappear or come out strange. To see how your article appears in an e-mail, send yourself a copy before you send it to an editor.

If you attach your article as a word-processor document, you can use a standard on-paper format, but don't send attachments unless an editor asks you to. Most editors will not open unsolicited attachments. Play it safe and ask first.

Going to Miss a Deadline?

If you run into problems, either with the story or an emergency in your life, and you know you won't be able to meet your deadline, contact the editor right away. He is counting on that piece to fill a space in the paper and may be in trouble if you don't tell him it's not coming.

Also call if you have questions or the story seems to be turning in a different direction from the one you agreed on. Don't annoy the editor by calling every day, but if you really need to talk about something, believe me, he would want you to call or send an e-mail rather than surprise him.

Exercises

• Clip out articles that you especially like and analyze what the writers have done. Mark the lead, nut graf, sub-topics, transitions, and the ending. Note how they attribute sources. In a feature, study how they use dialogue, settings, and sensory details. Just as artists learn by copying famous paintings, you can learn by imitating what the pros do.

• Write a first draft of an article. If you have an assignment for a newspaper, start writing. If you don't have an assignment, write a practice article which, with any luck, will soon be published. Because it's a draft, it doesn't have to be perfect, but do proofread and spell-check. We'll learn how to polish it up in the next chapter.

Chapter 8

Rewriting

Things move rapidly in the newspaper business. Sometimes you only have a few days, or even only one day, to write an article. Staff writers are usually expected to turn out at least one story a day. It may work out that they write one on Monday, none on Tuesday and three on Wednesday, gathering material in between, but they are expected to average at least five a week. Most of those stories are not big features or investigative pieces, just short workaday articles conveying information.

When you write that much that quickly, you get good at it, but, considering the pace, I'd be willing to bet big money most reporters would love to have another shot at their stories. I know I always felt that way. Upon reading it in print, I could see the clichés, the sentences that might have been written better, the weak transitions from concept to concept, the missing information, and myriad other problems that I would have fixed if the story hadn't been due in an hour.

As a freelancer, you have that second chance: Put it down for a day and go back and reread it, then fine tune it. You might do this twice, if time permits.

Perhaps you're thinking that it is the editor's job to strengthen your work and to find errors and correct them. Well, yes and no. Editors expect you to turn in clean, well-written copy with few mistakes. There will always be some things you don't see that an editor or proofreader will catch, but never turn in a story you haven't checked and rechecked. If you send an editor raw work that he has to spend a lot of time fixing, he will quickly decide that working with you is more trouble than it's worth.

Andrew Kiraly, managing editor of *Las Vegas CityLife*, speaks for all editors when he says, "Practice and polish; sloppy mistakes are a deal-killer."

When you think you are done with a piece, take the time to study the overall article with the eye of an editor. Do you have a catchy lead? Is it clear what this story is about? Does the order make sense, with clean transitions from one thought to another? Do you wrap it up with an ending that feels finished? Do you provide sources of additional information? Have you answered all the questions you promised to answer?

Before you send a story in, look carefully at what you say and how you say it. I like to compare it to looking through a camera lens. First you take the wide angle overall view, then focus in at medium range, then look through the telephoto, the long one bird-watchers use.

Wide Angle–What You Said

- Do you have a headline? Take time to write one, even if you worry the editor will end up using something else.
- Does the opening paragraph catch the reader's attention? Does it lead smoothly into the rest of the story?
- Did you follow up with an orienting paragraph that explains what the story is about?
- Have you placed a quote high up in the story?
- Did you cover the subject thoroughly?
- Did your ideas transition smoothly from one to another?
- Did you back up your opinions and observations with facts and examples?
- Did you unnecessarily repeat the same thing more than once?

• When you reach the end, does the story seem complete?

• Is there too much information or not enough, too many examples or too few?

• Are there questions you raise but don't answer?

• Do you provide resources the reader can use to find more information on the subject?

• Is the story you have written the one you pitched in your query and the one promised in the headline and in the lead?

• Are you sure of all your facts?

• Is the piece within 10 percent of the length the editor wants?

Medium Range—How You Said It

• Are there excess words that you can trim?

• Can you recast any sentences written in the passive voice, using stronger verbs?

• Do you need to vary the lengths of your sentences?

• Are you misplacing your modifiers or dangling your participles? ("Coming down the hillside, the little white church was clearly visible." Wow, a traveling church.)

• Are there terms or acronyms that you need to explain?

• Are there general words that could be more specific, replacing *trees* with *aspens* for instance?

• Do you use the same word more than once in a paragraph or open two paragraphs in a row with the same phrase?

Telephoto—The Myriad Details

• Check your spelling. Remember, don't trust the spell checker on your computer. It won't catch *too* when you meant *two*.

• Double-check dates, Web addresses, and phone numbers. The worst mistake you can make is to misspell a name. I had a journalism teacher who automatically gave us an F on any article that came in with a misspelled name. It's *that* important.

• Make sure your subjects and verbs agree. This can get a lot trickier than "he don't" or "I seen," especially in complex sentences. In many cases, if you temporarily remove the intervening words, mistakes become quite clear.

• Use parallel construction. Use the same grammatical construction when using words or groups of words which do the same work. This will often come up when a conjunction such as *and, but, for,* or *nor* is used in a sentence to tie two phrases together. For instance, change: Bob entered timidly, Sam with boldness; to: Bob entered timidly, Sam boldly.

• Check your word choices. Some commonly misused words: *Lay* versus *lie*; *I, me,* and *myself*; *alright* or *all right*; *among* or *between*; *it's* and *its*. When in doubt, check your dictionary or the *Associated Press Stylebook*.

• Cut unnecessary words. Can you *stand* any way but *up*?

• Check your punctuation.

• Watch for clichés—phrases that have been overused to the point of becoming trite or meaningless. There are too many to list, but *slow as molasses* and *a month of Sundays* come to mind.

• Look for slang words that some readers won't understand or that don't fit the tone of the newspaper. Explain the first and remove the second.

• Look for fancy words that should be replaced with common words. Replace *interrogate* with *ask*, *domicile* with *home*, *altercation* with *fight*.

• Locate and correct typos.

Word processing by computer has eased a lot of the writing process, but it has also introduced a new kind of error that is easy to miss. You think you have cut out a passage and replaced it with another, but later find remnants of the old words still there or parts of the replacement lines missing or out of order. You may have copied the same lines into two different places. You can also get into trouble with numbered lists when you decide to rearrange them and forget to change the numbers. Or maybe you marked a word to check on later or gave yourself several choices, fully intending to delete all but the correct word, but forgot to do so.

This is why you need a fresh eye to proofread. If you have time, let your story sit for a few days, then take another look. Usually, you will find something else to fix. If you have any doubts, ask someone else to check it.

But I Thought It Was Great

Another rewrite may come later, after the editor sees it. We all hope that the editor will read our story, declare it perfect and publish it immediately, but unfortunately no piece of writing is ever perfect. In fact, before you read this book, it will have gone through many revisions, and you will probably still find an error or two.

Although perfection is unlikely, try to get as close as you can. The guidelines for the *Chicago Reader* are particularly straightforward about this situation: "We have a healthy appreciation for writerly idiosyncrasies but little patience for lazy reporting or bad logic... Stories that need a lot of editing tend to migrate to editors' back burners."

Most of us dread telephone calls from an editor that begin, "About your story...." I know I do. The editor has questions and/or changes he wants to make. Like a root canal, there's no way around it. Just as the dentist finds the holes in your teeth, a good editor finds the holes in your stories. They may be minor, such as your source's title at the company where he works, or a big problem, such as you didn't include quotes or information from the other side of a controversial subject. This means you'll have to go back to your notes or do more research to fill in the blanks.

As you become a more experienced writer, you'll become adept at anticipating these problems in advance and providing the correct material in your first draft.

Sometimes the questions are more of a clearing-up, making-sure nature: Did he really say that? This sentence isn't clear; do you mean this or do you mean that? Can you give me a little bit more on this topic, maybe a sentence explaining the process?

Sometimes the editor will want you to make major changes. He may ask for a new or different emphasis, that you cut 200 words, make bullet points out of your paragraphs, or pull out some of the material for a sidebar. In other words, he may ask you to rewrite the whole darned thing. Count to ten, go for a walk, say the Serenity Prayer or whatever it takes to calm yourself, then do it. Most of the changes he wants will probably make your story stronger. Besides, the editor is the boss. You hate working with him? Don't pitch him any more stories. That's the beauty of freelancing.

The editor may have written a new lead or made other changes and wants to know if you approve. Generally, you don't have much leverage here. If the facts are accurate, you should probably say yes. Although recently an editor stuck two clichés in the first paragraph of my revised lead and I protested. He changed them.

Some editors will not ask the writer to revise the story or to approve the changes that are made. They'll just have their way with it. This can happen for a variety of reasons, ranging from a story that needs more work than the editor feels the writer can do to an editor who simply wants to impose his own style on every story.

Often the editor feels there isn't time to involve the writer in making the changes. Luckily, the development of the Internet has helped in this area. An editor who might never have had time to make a copy of the story, put it in the mail and wait for your response can e-mail the revised story for you to read and return the same day. Good editors will do this if they have made substantial changes.

It hurts when you open the newspaper and barely recognize your own article. Not only did they change your headline, but it isn't the lead you wrote. Or the whole thing has been reorganized. Unfortunately, once it's published, there's not much you can do about it. Do not telephone the editor to discuss it unless, in changing the story, he has changed the facts and made your story inaccurate or misleading. Then he deserves to be alerted to it and may need to run a correction to protect you and the paper from angry readers.

When you find that the editor has drastically changed your story without telling you in advance, set it aside for a few days until you can look at it calmly, then compare your manuscript with the published version to see how it was changed and try to understand why. If the story is shorter, did you turn it in at the length requested or hope they'd make it fit somehow? Does the reorganization make it clearer? Do the paragraphs flow more smoothly? Did the editor insert explanations for technical terms or jargon? Did he fix your spelling errors? Did he change your numbers, dates, addresses and other bits of information to conform with newspaper style? Did he take out all your *Mr.*, *Mrs.*, and *Miss* uses? Although these titles were common years ago, newspapers rarely use them now. Nor do they include titles such as Dr. on second reference, preferring to use just the last name.

By analyzing the ways the editor has changed your story, you may learn a great deal. In some cases what you learn is that you don't want to work for that editor again, but most editors are honest workers trying to put out the best publication they can. Because they are not personally invested in the story, they can make improvements that the writer simply cannot see.

"Don't get married to your words. If an editor doesn't like them and cuts them, so be it. Learn from those changes instead of resenting them," says Sue Harris, arts editor for the *Provincetown Banner*.

As the *Baptists Today* guidelines state, "Don't be overly possessive or defensive about your writing. Even the best writers benefit from critique. Let others help you improve your work. In other words, if you are unwilling to trust the material to the editor's red pen, please don't submit it." Amen.

Revisions

Let's look at the most likely reasons you will need to revise your story:

It's too Short or too Long

Sometimes you just can't seem to make your story fit into the allotted number of words, characters or inches allowed. Rarely, you won't have enough material. In that case, take another look at your original questions. Have you answered them all thoroughly? Are there anecdotes you can include to fill out the story? Do you need to do another interview to provide a more balanced view?

More often, you'll have way too much. You can try begging the editor for more space. Once in a blue moon, your request will be granted. The editor has only so much space for your story and readers only have so much attention span.

"But it's all good," you say. "I can't cut my story." Yes, you can. One thing I learned while working as an editor was that every word is expendable. Far better you trim your story now than an editor cuts it an hour before it goes to press, deleting the last paragraphs or trimming a whole section, with no regard to what is left unsaid.

Years ago when I worked on the copy desk for the *Hayward Daily Review*, one of my tasks—in addition to answering telephone calls from disgruntled readers who had not gotten their papers—was proofreading the Sunday sections. In those days, we were still drawing page layouts on paper. Strips of type were pasted onto heavier paper boards. We marked corrections and cuts with blue pencils that wouldn't show when the pages were photographed for printing. Each Sunday, I faced dozens of strips of type hanging off the pages. These were good stories, but I had to cut them—literally—until they fit. The easiest way was from the bottom.

Today, most of the cutting is done on the computer screen. Computer layout makes it possible to adjust the spacing of the type and photos to squeeze in a few more words, but stories still get trimmed, especially if you turn in more words than requested.

It's better to do it yourself than to leave the job to someone who is on deadline and doesn't care as much about what you have written. Here are some tips for finding what to cut:

• Look for redundancies. Have you said the same thing more than once? Have you quoted two people saying essentially the same thing? It is not necessary to include every quote that you have or even to quote every source. It has often been said that the writer should know considerably more than goes into the final draft. A lot will have to be left out, but it's there as background if you need it.

• Look for sections that stray off the topic. Your story is about a resort in Waikiki, but toward the end you write a few paragraphs about places you could visit in other parts of Oahu. Cut!

• Look for wordiness. Straightforward sentences with specific nouns and active verbs will speed your story along as well as shortening it. Don't lard your writing up with unnecessary adjectives, adverbs, and phrases. Consider every descriptive word. Do you need *in the interest of* or can you write *to*?

• Trim the conclusion. It's good to finish with a paragraph that makes your point or sums up what you have said, but don't linger too long. As in *Hamlet*, once most of the major characters have killed each other, there isn't much left to say.

You may reach a point where there doesn't seem to be any more to cut and yet you're still over the required length. This is the toughest part. Prioritize what you have and delete the sections with the lowest priority. It's all you can do. If you're within 10 percent of your word-count goal, surrender and let the editor make the final cut.

You Buried Your Lead

In fiction, sometimes the real story starts somewhere around the second chapter and everything leading up to it is just introduction and stage-setting. The same thing happens in newspaper articles. Perhaps the statement that tells what this article is about is not high up in your article but in a paragraph down the page a bit. Try starting there and see if your story takes on new life.

You've Gotten off Track

Does the body of your story deliver what your query letter said it would? Or have you written a different article than you promised? You need either to rewrite to fit the original concept or convince the editor that you need to go in a different direction.

You Raised a Question but Forgot to Answer It

Have you heard the saying that if there's a gun in Act I, somebody had better use it by the end of Act III? The same idea applies to newspaper articles. If you say there are several good reasons whitening toothpastes don't work, you need to tell us what those reasons are. If you say, "Mike opened the door and was shocked at what he saw," you have to tell us what he saw and why it was shocking. If you claim there are ten easy ways to cheat on your taxes, then you must list ten ways. People will actually count to see if they're all there.

What If You Do Your Best and the Editor Still Doesn't Like It?

Sometimes a writer and editor will never reach agreement on how an article should be written. In magazines, the writer is often entitled to a *kill fee*, a percentage of the originally promised payment. Most newspapers don't do this. They don't have the time or the staff to deal with it. Luckily it rarely becomes an issue. The editor already knows on the basis of your query and clips that you can do the job, so it comes down to a matter of compromise. You make the changes he wants; he makes compromises; a version of the story goes to press; and you get a check. With any luck, the resulting product will be an article you're both proud of. If not, take your money and move on to the next assignment.

If your story never runs in the newspaper that originally assigned it and you have not sold them all rights to it, you are free to offer it to another publication. With luck, the new market will buy it for more money than you would have made at the first paper.

They're Only Criticizing Your Words, Not You

Don't take a request for a rewrite as a sign that you're a lousy writer. Take it as an opportunity to make a good story even better. Be grateful for the opportunity to polish your work, and let the editor help you do it. A well-honed story will make both you and the newspaper look good. It will also give you a great clip to use with future queries. And the people you write about may frame your story and put it on the wall. God forbid you walk into a store someday, see your article over the cash register and find a big mistake in it. Be thankful for revisions and for the editors who make you do them.

Exercises

• Take another look at the article you wrote for the last chapter—or another story that you have already written, then revise and polish it until it's the best it can possibly be.

• Take a published 1,000-word article by someone else on any subject. As you read it, highlight the most important elements of the text. Now, just as an exercise, not for publication, rewrite the article in 500 words.

Chapter 9

Getting Paid and Getting More Assignments

In the preceding chapters, we have studied markets, ideas, queries, research, interviews, writing, and rewriting. You may have some articles well on their way to publication. Maybe you've had some setbacks. Or maybe you haven't started yet. Don't worry. This is not a race. The most important quality in this business of freelancing is persistence. If you keep at it, you will succeed.

However, there's more to being a freelance writer than just writing. It's the business part, all the things that aren't writing, that causes some talented scribes to throw up their hands in disgust. In fact, congratulate yourself if you have made it this far. I have had students who quit after hearing what they need to do to sell their stories. They just want to follow their muse and write. The catch is that they also would like to be published and make some money.

Speaking of money...

Okay, I Wrote the Thing; How Do I Get Paid?

In a perfect world, you write your article and a check arrives along with the letter of acceptance. It happens that way in the movies. In real life, however, the editor is drowning in e-mails, faxes, snail-mail, and phone calls and is trying to write stories, edit stories, lay out pages, supervise writers, obey the demands of management, and deal with the readers, all at the same time. Getting a check to you may be way at the bottom of the to-do list. It may not even be on the list unless you take action.

It may be that the newspaper pays upon publication, which means you have to wait for the article to run. Getting paid on acceptance is better because you get paid sooner. However, many newspapers pay on publication, settling accounts after their advertisers pay for their ads. Writers must share the revenue flow with the paper's printers, computer technicians, photographers, graphic artists, and other business people.

Some publications have well-organized systems for paying writers. Others don't, so it's up to you to make sure that that last important bit of business gets taken care of.

The editor rarely writes the check but often authorizes payment. He may have a form to send to the accounting department or to his boss for approval. Or drum roll—he may be waiting for you to send an invoice. Long ago, I waited until a couple of months slipped by after I published an article in the *San Jose Mercury News.* When I called my editor to inquire where the payment was, he asked if I had sent an invoice. A *what*? It turns out that nothing got paid without an invoice at the *Merc* and that is true today at many other newspapers. Besides, sending an invoice makes you look professional.

How do you generate an invoice? Office supply stores sell forms, and you can find templates for invoices on most word-processing programs. These are more oriented to other types of businesses, but you can make them work. You can also make up your own simple form that provides all the basic information. Place your name, address, phone number and e-mail address at the top. Put a date on it, type the name and address of the publication, then list the article or articles, the dates they ran and the amount of money you expect to be paid.

For example, I recently turned in an invoice to *Northwest Senior News* that read in part:

Pirate's Plunder feature—600 words at $.12/word= $72.00
Senior Discounts column—600 words at $.12/word= $72.00
Open mic item—150 words at $.12/word= $18.00
Three photos at $7= $21.00
Expenses: mileage—13 miles at 29 cents/mile= $3.77
Total due=$186.77

That's all there is to it. I knew from experience that about two weeks after that issue came out, I would receive my check.

Enclose a self-addressed stamped envelope with your invoice at first. Later on, you may find that the newspaper will provide the envelope and the stamp.

Some writers add a statement to the effect that they expect this bill to be paid within 30 days or 60 days or whatever. Some threaten to charge interest on overdue payments. I simply thank the publication for the assignment and "for prompt payment." Follow your instinct on this. You don't want to come off as cranky, but you do want to show that you're serious about getting paid on time.

Most publishers are pretty good about payment. If for some reason, months go by and a couple of polite letters or phone calls don't bring you any money, it's time to take tougher action. First, call the accounting department and ask to speak to the person who issues checks for freelance articles. If that doesn't get you paid, you might contact the National Writers Union, which has had a lot of success in forcing reluctant publishers to pay. You can also take the publication to small claims court, but you need to weigh the amount of money owed against the effort and time it would take. Meanwhile, don't write anything else for that publication. They may just be poorly organized, or they may be about to go out of business, taking your unpaid debt with them.

Clips, Clips, Clips

The more clips you have, the more evidence that you are an experienced writer who has proven you can do the job.

Online Clips

If your story is published on the Internet, just click on the website and print it out as many times as you like or make several photocopies. Keep a list of the links for your online stories so that you can include them in e-mail queries and other correspondence. Check the links occasionally to make sure your story hasn't been moved to another address or deleted. In fact, just in case, you may want to copy the story into your own website or make a PDF clip file so that if your story disappears from the newspaper's website, you can still provide a link to use with future queries.

Printed Copies

To obtain printed copies, it's a little trickier. Don't expect the newspaper to send you a copy. If you plan to write regularly for this publication, you should subscribe and that is how you'll get your clip. If you are already published with them, ask if they offer complimentary subscriptions to regular contributors. Many newspapers do. If not, the subscription is tax-deductible, and it's important that you keep up with what they're publishing.

If you live where the newspaper is published, you can go to the office and pick up a stack of papers. If you have friends or relatives who subscribe, have them save the paper for you. Lacking these options, ask the editorial secretary or the newspaper's librarian to mail you a copy. They may ask you to send a self-addressed stamped envelope. Don't complain that this is unfair; just do it.

Make several photocopies to use for future queries. You also may want to start a scrapbook, what old-time journalists used to call a "string book." Not only is this good for your ego, but it's a handy way to show off your work to editors, agents, colleagues, students, doubting relatives and anyone else who might be interested. Plus, you always know where you can find a copy of your story.

Every article you publish is another step toward establishing yourself as a freelancer. Save your clips. Not only will they help you get more assignments, but they all have the potential to be sold again or reworked into new stories.

Even if you don't make much money at first, you can use your clips to move up the newspaper ranks. David L. Ulin, book editor of the *L.A. Times,* started writing book reviews for a local arts publication. It didn't pay any money, but he got clips to use when he approached higher-level markets. "I kept sending to the next notch up the food chain," he says. In addition to publishing in the *New York Times Book Review,* the

Atlantic Monthly, Newsday and *The Nation,* Ulin has edited two Los Angeles literary anthologies and published his own book, *The Myth of Solid Ground: Earthquakes, Prediction and the Fault Line Between Reason and Faith.* It all started with those first unpaid book reviews.

Copyright

In the United States, you own the copyright to whatever you write as soon as you commit it to paper or computer file. It is yours to sell or give away—even without officially registering it. You can leave it to your heirs when you die.

As of 1998, the Sonny Bono Copyright Term Extension Act extends the length of copyright protection. For works created after January 1, 1978, copyright lasts for the life of the author plus an additional 70 years. For works published between 1923 and 1978, it used to be 28 years with possible renewal for another 28. Now those earlier works can be renewed for 67 years.

Registering a copyright gives you added legal protection in the event of a challenge. As of this writing the fee to register a copyright in the U.S. is about $45. Because you already own the copyright and the costs can add up, register only your most important works. One way to save time and money is to bundle a group of articles into a collection and register them as one entity. For more information on copyrights, visit the Library of Congress copyright office website: copyright.gov.

Can I Really Sell This Article Somewhere Else?

Because of government copyright laws, you own every piece you write and you can sell or license rights to this work in many different ways. For instance, you might sell "first serial rights" that would allow a particular publication to be the first to publish your article. You might even sell "North American first serial rights" to one publisher and retain the right to allow another publisher to be the first to publish the work in another area of the world.

It is common to sell "one-time rights." This is the right to publish the article just one time, but not necessarily the first time.

With the advent of electronic publishing via the Web and other ways, more and more publishers are requiring that they be allowed to purchase "all rights." This means just what it says, that publisher has all rights to your piece. Try not to sell all rights.

If they insist on buying all rights or treating your story as a *work for hire*, which means that they consider it their property in the same way that they own the works of employees who write for them. Try to talk them out of it, but if they won't budge, take a minute to consider whether it's worth fighting over. In many cases, the story that you craft for a particular newspaper won't work anyplace else without a complete rewrite anyway. If the money is good or you need the clips—or it just sounds like fun—go ahead, but know what you're doing. If you don't want to give up all rights, tell them so and be ready to walk away if they won't settle for less.

If you don't sell all rights, the story is yours to sell again. Someday you might even want to publish a collection of your best articles in a book.

Even if you retain resale rights to your story, you should not offer it to another newspaper in the same city or to a newspaper that reaches the same audience. But you may offer it to another paper in another market. Say you published it the first time in Tampa, Florida. Will the story also work in Boise or Los Angeles? Will it be of interest to a special-interest newspaper, such as a religious paper or a trade paper? Is there an online outlet that might want to buy it?

Send the new market a copy of the story and offer it as a reprint. You should always mention that it was published before and where, but you can resell the same story as many times as you can convince someone to buy it.

Perhaps this story is generally interesting to another paper but needs some work to fit their focus. Revise it to fit their needs and sell it again. For example, you might be able to sell the same basic information on accounting to several trade papers serving different types of businesses. If the focus has substantially changed, this is a new story for which you can again offer first rights or even all rights.

One of the frustrating aspects of freelancing for smaller newspapers is that the editor may not even know what rights she is claiming when she buys a story from you. Major papers send you a contract that spells out the rights in enough dizzying detail to please any attorney, but I have encountered smaller papers that don't have a specific policy on copyright. One editor I have worked with in recent years says, "Ah, don't worry about it. Just don't write for our competitors."

Always ask what rights a particular publication buys. If the answer is fuzzy, tell them you are offering one-time rights. Write "One-time rights" at the top of your story as well as mentioning it in a letter or e-mail to the editor. That way, you know for sure that you have the right to resell that story somewhere else.

Reuse Your Research

Maybe you sold all rights or you have used up all possible markets for this particular story, but you have a pile of information, more than you were able to use, and you're still interested in the subject. Why not write a different piece? Back at that river where you wrote about the pollution, did you collect some information on the local fishing industry? Maybe you'd like to interview some fishermen, even spend a day on the river with them, and write a new story. The pollution can be a small piece of that story, too, but this one would look more at the fishermen's lifestyle, the history of local fishing, and the kinds of boats and fishing gear they use. Or you could profile one of the guys on the boat or write about how to purchase a fishing boat or....

How about a sequel? Is there a new development that you could offer as a follow-up story to the publication that ran the first one?

Sally Abrahms started her career with one article on parental kidnapping. That led to more and more related articles. "I just kept taking the subjects and parlaying them into more markets," she said. Eventually she wrote a book, but she didn't stop there. She sold more articles and opinion pieces on related topics. "I just spun it to death," she says.

If you think of writing as a business, the articles you write and the information you collect are your inventory. Keep track of what you've got in stock and look for ways to sell it again and again.

What about Syndication?

If you pay attention to newspaper bylines, you will see listings for various syndicates. Copley News Service, Catholic News Service, Tribune Media Services, Hispanic Link News Services, and King Features Syndicate are among the better-known companies. Syndicates buy articles, columns, cartoons, puzzles and other works and sell them to newspapers. The "Dear Abby" column is syndicated. "Doonesbury" is syndicated. So is Dr. Ruth's sex advice column.

Syndicates handle all the marketing and pay the writer a flat fee or a percentage of what newspapers pay them. They also control all the rights to your work, but that isn't all bad because it frees you to focus on your writing and let someone else worry about the business end.

However, before you start making a list of syndicates to approach, here's the tough part. The established syndicates rarely add new writers and almost never consider writers who haven't already developed a following by publishing in major newspapers or magazines. They also tend to favor ongoing columns and cartoons, although some syndicates will accept one-time pieces.

If you're new in the business, the odds aren't good. In *Successful Syndication,* Michael Sedge writes that King Features receives more than 6,000 submissions a year. Out of that 6,000, only *three* are chosen for syndication. If you believe you deserve to be one of the three, put together several samples of your work and pitch them with a query letter in the same way you would pitch an article to an individual newspaper. After all, you can't win if you don't ante up.

Self-syndication is another option, especially with a column. Put together several sample columns, biographical information and a photo of yourself, then offer it to all the papers that seem likely to be interested. In exchange for a small fee, you will send them a new column ever day, week, month or whatever you agree on. It can work. Writers have done it and made themselves household names. Bob Rossner, who writes a business advice column called "Working Wounded," claims more than 100 newspaper clients, and Tim Carter's "Ask the Builder" column has had similar success. But for most of us, self-syndication means we will spend more time marketing than writing and make relatively little money for the effort. On the plus side, if you self-syndicate, you earn all the money and retain total control of your work. If you dream of appearing in papers all over the country, it's an option to consider.

While you're perusing the bylines in newspapers, you will find Associated Press and its siblings, such as Gannett News Service or the New York Times Service. These are wire services. As with the major syndicates, freelance publication through these companies is possible but unlikely. They obtain their articles, usually staff-written, from newspapers that subscribe to their service or are owned by the same company. Each day, they send a menu of completed stories to their member newspapers. The editor picks the ones that most fit his needs, finds a place for them in the paper and formats them to match that paper's style and layout. The writer has nothing to do with it.

If you are lucky enough to publish in a major newspaper, such as the *New York Times* and your story goes out to the wire service with the staff-written stories and other papers decide to pick it up, you could have clips from all over the country or even the world, which would give a nice boost to your career. However, you can't control whether or not this happens, and, because these papers usually purchase all rights, it's likely you won't make another cent from this exposure.

Ultimately, all you can do is write the best story you can and sell it to the best publication you can get into, gradually moving up the ranks as you build your career.

Once You Have Your Foot in the Door

Ideally, by now you have contacted at least one newspaper editor. Best case, you have an assignment that you have done or are working on. Even if all you have achieved is a rejection, it's a start. The key to succeeding as a freelancer is becoming a regular contributor in several markets. You want to become one of those people whom an editor calls with assignments and who can obtain an assignment with a quick phone call or e-mail. You want to be part of the team, without the entanglements (or the benefits) of a job (although it's nice if you're invited to the annual Christmas party).

It's important to have more than one regular freelance outlet because publishing is a constantly-changing business. Papers fold or run into financial trouble, editors leave or new publishers change the focus, and suddenly you don't get any more assignments. There was a time when I contributed steadily to three newspapers where I was proud to see my byline. Then two of the three went out of business in the same month, leaving me with the least dependable of the three and a big hole in my income. So, as they say in the stock market, diversify.

How Do You Get on the List of Beloved Freelancers?

Follow-up is the key. If an editor says no to your first idea, come up with another one. If an editor says yes to your first idea, come up with another one. In fact, once you have sold a couple of articles to the same editor, there's nothing wrong with typing up several ideas and trying to get assignments for them all at once. You might also ask if there's anything they wish they could find somebody to write. And then respond, "How many words and when do you need it?"

Another technique Jennifer Meacham uses is to send a copy of an article she has published elsewhere that the editor might find interesting. She sends an e-mail saying, "I just finished research on this. I thought it might be helpful to you." That way, even when she isn't pitching a specific article, she keeps in touch.

Although the world is full of people who want to be writers, newspaper editors have trouble finding writers who can actually deliver a well-written article on time. If you are one of those writers, they'll love you. Once you make the list of proven freelancers, the editor will turn to you again and again.

Most newspapers these days are owned by big corporations that publish several newspapers. The editors of these newspapers often share articles, so your piece may appear in more than one paper, and if you're lucky, you'll get paid a little more each time it appears. Even if you don't make more money, the exposure will help your career. Also, if one editor in a chain likes your work, he may refer you to the other editors. Soon they'll be calling you with assignments, too.

If you really want to write for a particular publication, the worst thing you can do is disappear. If they encourage you in any way to try again, do it before your name fades from memory. Keep trying until the editor asks you to quit or until you decide it's not going to work. If you have been rejected three times by the same publication, step back and think about it. Does your style just not fit? Are you missing the point somewhere?

When you do get your work accepted, don't immediately decide that you and the editor are now best friends. Keep the relationship professional. Don't drop in, call, write or fax the editor every day, and don't call the editor by her first name until she calls you by yours. But do try to have something under consideration or be working on something for them on a regular basis. As you look for article ideas, keep the publication in mind.

Develop a Specialty

Just starting out, you may want to write about whatever intrigues you or offers itself as subject matter. Over time you may find yourself writing about a particular subject more than once because that's what you know about and are interested in or because that's where you found work. Either way, by the time you have accumulated several related clips and fat folders full of information, you are in fact becoming a freelancer with a specialty.

That's what happened to Sally Abrahms. She hadn't planned to specialize in family legal issues, but one article led to another, and editors started seeing her as an expert.

Other writers develop several related specialties. Jennifer Meacham, for example, writes about diverse subjects under the general heading of business.

David L. Ulin prefers not to be chained to one specialty, but most of his newspaper work, which started with book reviews, has centered around books, authors, and the arts. He warns that a specialty can turn into a straitjacket if editors start to think you can't do anything else. "Use it, but try and push the boundaries a little bit as well."

Although you can write about anything that interests you, having a specialty can be a real plus. Your clips, contacts, and knowledge will give added power to your queries. Based on what you have already published, editors may come to you with assignments. It will be easier to do the stories because you are building on knowledge you already have. When your byline appears regularly in the same field, people get to know your name, which leads to more opportunities, not just for writing but for speaking, teaching, books, and more.

Like Meacham, you don't have to have only one specialty. You can claim several areas that interest you and pursue them. As we discussed in the chapter on ideas, think about what you know. Perhaps you are already an expert without even realizing it.

Specializing can make freelancing easier, but it's like dating. Don't settle down until you've found the right fit.

Chapter 10

The Business of Being a Freelance Writer

As a freelance writer, you are in business. Writing articles for newspapers isn't the kind of business that requires you to incorporate or obtain a license from the city to work out of your home. If you decided to publish your own newspaper and started having lots of people come to your office, that would be a different story. With freelancing, nobody needs to know what you're doing sitting at the computer in your pajamas at noon.

The one exception is the Internal Revenue Service. If you make any money with your writing, you should declare it on your income tax return. If you make more than $600 from any one publication, they will file a Form 1099 with the government, so the feds know what you earned and can check to see if you have reported it.

In tax terms, you are the sole proprietor of a small business and need to file a form called Schedule C. That form calls for a detailed accounting of your expenses and income.

Keep records of all your expenses and retain the receipts. If you don't keep track during the year, you won't have the information you need to fill out the form.

Use whatever system works for you. Some people simply write all of their expenses in their datebooks, along with their activities for the day. Others enter them on a spreadsheet or use an accounting program such as Quicken.

I write everything in a bound account book, with columns for income, mileage, office supplies, Internet fees, telephone bills, photo developing, subscriptions to publications, and other writing-related expenses. I keep all my receipts for the year in one big envelope.

At the end of the year, I tally the columns and transfer the totals to my Schedule C. If my husband and I are ever audited, I have a record and proof of everything we claimed on our return.

If questioned by the IRS, you need to prove that you are legitimately working as a writer. That means you must show that you are writing and trying to sell what you write. Otherwise, it's considered a hobby and the expenses are not deductible. Keep your manuscripts, keep records of what you submit, and keep the responses you get, including your rejection slips. Also keep calendars that show your appointments for interviews and meetings with editors.

Officially, you should show a profit three out of five years, but if you don't, nothing bad will happen to you if you can demonstrate what the IRS calls a "profit motive." You haven't become a household name yet, but you're trying.

If your writing really is just a hobby that you do occasionally for fun, forget Schedule C and simply list any money you make as "miscellaneous income." You cannot claim your expenses in that case any more than you can claim your golf course fees if you're not a professional golfer.

As a freelance writer, you may also be eligible to deduct expenses related to having an office in your home. To qualify, you need a space that you use for your writing. You can deduct a portion of your mortgage or rent, utilities and other expenses. It would be wise to talk it over with a tax professional to see if you qualify and if it is worthwhile taking this deduction. You may not need it for the first few years, plus it raises a red flag that can trigger audits.

In addition to helping with your taxes, keeping detailed financial records will help you analyze your profits and losses at the end of the year, showing where you need to work harder and where you are spending too much money for too little return. If you hope to make significant income from your writing, you really need to keep these records and treat your work as a business.

But here's another thought: Maybe you don't really want to make it a business. Maybe you just enjoy writing and publishing the occasional article, whether you get paid or not. Don't let anyone make you feel bad for that. Writing from the heart for one's own fulfillment is just as valid as writing for money. Although I often jokingly call myself a "crass commercial writer," the truth is that if I were a billionaire and didn't need to write for pay, I would still write because I enjoy it and because I feel as if I have something important to contribute to the world.

A Room of Your Own

Even if you don't have a separate office, you should have a space that is dedicated to writing, a place where you can set up your computer and spread out your papers. You'll need a telephone and Internet access in this work space.

A service such as a fiber-optic-based Digital Subscriber Line, which allows you to use one line for voice, fax and Internet all at the same time, might be a good investment.

If you don't have an answering machine or voice-mail service, get one. Imagine if a source you've been trying to reach for weeks calls while you're taking a shower, out shopping, at your day job, or otherwise unavailable. You may never get a chance to interview him.

Record a professional, non-gimmicky message and let the system be your secretary. If other people answer the telephone when you're not there, train them to take clear, readable messages. When you answer the telephone during working hours, identify yourself, so that sources know they have reached the right number. A professional greeting, such as "Good morning, this is Joe," also cues your friends and family that you are working.

If at all possible, find a workspace where you can close the door and concentrate on your writing. If you can't, you're in the same boat as most staff reporters. They don't usually have their own offices, just desks or cubicles, which they sometimes share with reporters who work other shifts. They learn to work in the midst of constant activity, with people talking, phones ringing, machines humming, and frequent interruptions.

Whether you have a whole room or just a desk in the corner, treat your writing as something important and devote a space in your home to it.

Tools of the Trade

We have mentioned the room, the desk, and the telephone. The other obvious piece of equipment you need is a computer. It can be a laptop or a desktop, a MAC or a PC. Microsoft Word is the most commonly used word-processing program, but any software that can save the file as RTF or "Rich Text Format" will work.

An Internet connection is essential, a necessary cost of doing business. Editors expect you to be able to send messages, stories and photos online. Try to avoid having to share a computer with anyone else in the household. This should be your own computer which you use for work.

The price of computers has gone down considerably. My first computer, a Radio Shack brand purchased in 1985, cost $1,500 and did not come with a monitor, printer, speakers, CD or DVD slots, or a modem. It had a clunky word-processing program called Volkswriter. But it worked. I wrote, I published, and I moved up to better computers. My current system cost less and has all the goodies.

Computers are fantastic time-savers. They allow you to type your story just once and revise it an infinite number of times. They help you do much of your research from home, and they let you communicate day or night with people all over the world. Buy the best system you can afford and take the time to learn to use it. Editors expect writers to be computer-savvy these days, so read software manuals, try all the features that apply to your writing and ask questions until you are at ease with it.

As helpful as they are, computers can also drive you crazy. They break down, lock up, acquire viruses and just plain quit, usually when you're in the middle of a major project on deadline. Save your work often and back up everything you write on CDs, a Zip drive, a flash drive or memory stick, or any other system that allows you to place a copy of your work somewhere other than your hard drive.

I recommend making two backup copies of everything. Keep one in your office and the other at a location other than your house in case, God forbid, the house burns down, a hurricane blows it apart or a burglar decides to steal your computer and all your CDs.

Here's a tip. If you're in a hurry or traveling and you've just written something you don't want to lose, e-mail a copy to yourself. Then, even if your computer blows up, you can access your story from another computer.

Viruses will eat your computer from the inside out. Invest in computer virus protection with Norton or Symantec or another reputable company and install a firewall. It's worth the expense.

Fitting Freelancing in with Your Day Job

For many writers, freelancing is a good way to combine work with family obligations. It is not by chance that 73 percent of the 600 freelance journalists surveyed by the American Society of Journalists and Authors in 2005 were female. The survey also showed that 65 percent were married and 57 percent had at least one child. There is no mention of how many might have other caregiving responsibilities such as an ailing spouse or an elderly parent, but these are also situations where one might not be able to take a regular job but could do an occasional freelance article.

Freelancing is also a good option for people dealing with illnesses or disabilities that prevent them from working full-time. Being able to write and publish during troubled times is good medicine. It keeps you in contact with the world, moves your career along, and makes you feel as if you are contributing something creative and useful to society.

Freelancing is also good for people like me and maybe you who simply prefer to be their own bosses, working in their own time and space and in their own way. We like the freedom of freelancing. If we want to sleep in, we do. If we want to write at midnight, we do. If we decide to work for three newspapers at once, we can.

However, it's not all fun and freedom. While it is possible to get enough freelance work to live on, and it is even possible to earn a fortune if you hit the right markets, it's not easy, especially if you are supporting a family. A father of four who had not yet published anything recently asked me if he could match the $50,000 annual income, plus benefits, that he gets from his government job. At the risk of losing a student, I had to tell him it was unlikely. He decided to keep writing anyway.

Freelancing does not offer health insurance, paid sick leave, or retirement plans, and you can't always count on a steady income. Assignments, publication, and payment are all sporadic. You may have six stories going one month and nothing the next. You may write a piece in December and get paid in February. It is difficult to write or even come up with ideas when all you can think about is how you will pay the mortgage next month, especially when other people are depending on your income. Thus many of us can only daydream about freelancing full-time. What you see in the movies and on TV is not realistic. There is no way "Sex and the City's" Carrie Bradshaw could have made a living on one freelance column for one New York newspaper.

But there is hope. If you become a regular contributor to several newspapers that pay well and/or if you find ways to resell every article several times, you can bring in a pretty good income.

"I'm not rich by any state of the imagination, but I do well for a freelancer, and I live a life that I enjoy," Jennifer Meacham says. These days she combines her newspaper work with magazine assignments and teaching, but it all started with articles for her high school newspaper.

If you keep writing and publishing, the checks will keep coming. It is possible that your columns or features will become so popular that editors start calling you. You will still have to find your own health insurance and save some money for times when you are unable to work due to illness or family emergencies. Unless you plan to work forever, you should also look into IRAs, investments, and other options to support you in your old age. Meanwhile, you're doing what you always wanted to do.

Should you quit your day job? Not yet, unless you have suddenly become independently wealthy, married a rich person, or gotten a six-figure publishing contract.

Most of us have regular jobs that we can't afford to give up. I won't lie to you; trying to write freelance articles while holding down a 9-to-5 job is challenging. You may not be able to do articles that require interviews or research that can only take place during the day. Travel, opinion, personal experience, personality profiles and many other types of articles can be done during the evenings and weekends, but you won't be able to interview business people, government officials, university professors and others who are only available while you're at work. I admit to occasionally sneaking freelance phone calls while the boss wasn't listening and faking illness or dentist's appointments to slip away for an interview, but I don't recommend it. It's too stressful, and you risk getting fired.

You might try to chisel out some daytime hours from your job. On one job, for example, I volunteered to work Wednesday nights in exchange for Wednesday mornings off. Later, when they started a Saturday shift, I volunteered right away to cover Saturdays in exchange for a weekday off. Can you get flex time, coming in later or earlier so that you have some daylight hours for interviews? You can always squeeze in some work during your lunch break, but it would be easier on your stomach to just eat lunch and relax. It's impossible to fully engage in an interview when you're watching the clock worrying about getting back to work on time.

So, if you are just starting out, don't quit your job. Do what you can to adjust the freelancing and the job to fit together as well as possible. If your freelance business is growing to the point where you have steady assignments and not enough time to do them, think about taking a part-time job. If you do decide to freelance full-time, stash enough to cover at least six months of living expenses in the bank and make sure you have health insurance before you quit your day job.

Should You Change Careers?

Here's another possibility: You love writing for newspapers and you're really starting to hate whatever else you've been doing for a living. Consider changing careers. Get an actual newspaper job with salary and benefits. You will probably not be hired as a staff reporter on any but the smallest newspapers without a college degree in journalism, mass communications, English, or some related field. But life is short; do what makes you happy. Start taking classes and keep freelancing. Look for entry-level job openings and for regular-contributor opportunities at papers in your area. Once you combine your practical experience with a college education, you'll have no trouble finding work at a newspaper.

When I started freelancing for the company that owned the *Saratoga News*, I had a journalism degree, but I hadn't worked at a regular job for seven years. In eight months, I went from freelancing to part-time reporter to full-time editor.

At the *Provincetown Banner*, arts editor Sue Harris says, "My current full-time arts writer/section assistant began as a freelancer, moved to part-time, then full-time reporter and then to the arts."

"We hardly ever accept unsolicited freelance material, and yet two of our four staff writers are former freelancers," writes Ted Taylor, editor of the *Eugene (Oregon) Weekly*.

Why not? Freelancers have proven they can do the work.

If you are seriously seeking a newspaper job, read the job listings at your state's newspaper association website. Also read the classified ads in *Editor and Publisher* magazine. In fact, read the help-wanted ads of every newspaper you pick up. And, being the resourceful writer that you are, if you notice that one of the regular writers' bylines hasn't shown up lately, consider sending your résumé because they might be looking for someone to take his place.

Meanwhile, keep plugging away. Building a freelance newspaper career takes time, patience and persistence. Most writers need to work their way up from small newspapers to big ones. Along the way, they will face rejections, revisions and frustration, but they will also find many rewards. After three decades in the business, I still get a kick out of seeing my stories in print. I love it when a person I interview tells me, "You rock!" or when readers say my articles opened up new possibilities for them. The paycheck isn't bad either.

Staff work on a newspaper is fast-paced and demanding and often extends beyond forty hours a week, but it is wonderfully satisfying. Not only do you get paid and published regularly, but you become a part of the community in a way you never were before. People know who you are and welcome you into their midst as the town scribe, the storyteller, the Writer.

Looking into the Future: Will Newspapers Disappear?

To insist that newspapers will continue on as they always have in this world of new media would be silly, but newspapers are not likely to disappear. As Brett Harvey, former executive director of the American Society of Journalists and Authors, says, "A newspaper is something you can read on the train; you can't really do that with your laptop."

Economically, however, newspaper companies are seeing a need to adapt. Print readership has dropped while online readership has increased. A November 2005 Nielsen//NetRatings study showed that one out of four Internet users had visited an Internet news site in the previous month. "This research follows on the heels of last week's news of the recent six-month decline in average weekday print circulation among America's top 20 largest newspapers, as reported by the Audit Bureau of Circulations." That same study showed that "among online adults who read either a print or online newspaper, 22 percent shifted their readership preferences from offline to online sources. The majority of readers, 71 percent, still prefer print newspapers while 7 percent divide their time evenly between the two sources."

Publishers of newspapers are now expanding into websites, blogs, podcasts, and vodcasts (video newscasts). You can get your news on PDAs, cell phones, laptops, and other media, as well as newspapers.

In an article titled "Adapt or Die" in the *American Journalism Review*, Rachel Smolkin notes that the main product is still information but how that information will be transmitted to readers is in transition, especially at the big metropolitan dailies. Quoting a Newspaper Association of America study on the changes in newspapers, Smolkin notes, "Old-school newspaper aficionados should bring along their decoders; instead of stories and readers, we now have 'content' and 'audience'; newspapers and their sister publications are 'products' that together create a 'portfolio.' And news itself is passé: We're in the information business now."

What does this mean for freelancers? Should we forget newspapers and start a blog instead? No. At the core of it all, the newspaper is still there. Community newspapers and special-interest papers will continue publishing far into the future. Even if they do stretch out into other media, the newspapers aren't folding, they're diversifying. Once upon a time, people could buy just one kind of Ford and it came in one color, black. Now we have all kinds of cars in every possible color, but we're still driving cars, not spaceships.

Likewise, newspapers are evolving but not going away. Editors will continue to need good writers with strong ideas, writers who can gather information and turn it into publishable articles. Even if your writing is now called "content" instead of "copy," editors are still looking for it. And readers are still reading it.

In practical terms, it does mean that the article you sell to your local newspaper could also end up on the Internet or on someone's iPod. Judging from the editors surveyed for this book, you probably won't get any extra money for this. It's considered part of the package.

Computerization has also had an effect on the way articles are written. In general, stories are shorter than they used to be, partly because news space and attention spans have shrunk, but also because people don't want to read long articles on a computer screen. They prefer short pieces that they can read in one sitting. They look for links to related sites for more information. More and more print articles refer readers to the publication's website for the rest of the story or to other sites for resource lists, commentary and other features. Writers are encouraged to break stories into smaller pieces, sometimes separating information out into two or three sidebars.

But the Internetization of newspapers isn't necessarily a bad thing. You're communicating with more people more quickly. Your stories can be read all over the world, they stay around longer than the newsprint version, and it's easy to e-mail online clips to editors when you're looking for more work. Many of the new outlets also provide an opportunity for readers to comment, establishing a dialogue that goes beyond the initial article. The industry is changing, but freelance writers will still be a valued part of it.

Resources for Freelance Writers

Resources to help you find markets for your writing

American Directory of Writer's Guidelines, Quill Driver Books. This annual is a collection of more than 1,700 publishers' actual guidelines for freelancers. These guidelines are written by the editorial staff at the individual periodical explaining what this publication is looking for from freelancers. It is a great place to browse for freelancing ideas. Contact information for each editor and publisher is included along with a topic index so you can zero in on publications that are interested in the subject you are writing about.

Association of Alternative Newsweeklies, aan.org. Many metropolitan areas have weekly papers that focus on news and entertainment with a hip, youthful twist. They are especially open to freelance articles, and free copies are usually available all over town.

Business journals, bizjournals.org. This is the website for American City Business Journals, publishers of localized newspapers covering business in more than 40 major U.S. cities.

Black press, BlackPressUSA.com represents more than 200 African-American community newspapers, with direct links to their sites.

Catholic archdiocesan newspapers. See catholicpress.org for the paper serving the Catholic churches where you live. Other denominations have their own newspapers. Search for information online. You can probably find free copies at the churches in your area.

Editor and Publisher International Year Book. This book costs several hundred dollars, and the CD-ROM version costs even more, so you'll want to look for it at the library, but it lists every general-interest newspaper and some specialized newspapers in the United States and beyond. Contact names, deadlines and other information are provided. Look for more information at editorandpublisher.com.

Ethnic newspapers, allied-media.com is the website for Allied Media Group, a good source to find newspapers focusing on Hispanics, African Americans and other racial and ethnic groups.

Jewish newspapers, jewishlink.net. Offers hundreds of links to newspapers and magazines.

Journalism jobs, journalismjobs.com. Here you'll find hundreds of listings, many of them for staff positions, but also included are freelance opportunities with good information on what the editors want and how to approach them.

International newspapers, inkpot.com/news. There's a whole world of English-language newspapers beyond the boundaries of the United States. This site will help you find them.

New America Media, NewAmericaMedia.org. This organization produces news and investigative articles which it sells to newspapers. Begun under the name Pacific News Service as an independent voice during the Vietnam War, today NAM focuses on diversity, not just in ethnicity, but in age and economic status.

News Directory from Electronic Library, newsd.com. Lists newspapers and magazines by subject and location.

Newslink.org. All sorts of newspapers are listed here in user-friendly fashion, with links that will take you directly to the newspaper itself.

Newspaper Association of America, naa.org. Click on "Membership Info" and scroll down to the member list for links to newspapers in every U.S. state.

New York Times op-ed guidelines–nytimes.com/pages/opinion.

Online Newspapers, onlinenewspapers.com. This site can lead you to Internet newspapers from all over the world.

Opinion-pages.org/cgi-bin/monitor/texis-cgi/webinator/ search/?pr=db. Search by topic in international newspapers.

Parenting Publications of America, parentingpublications.org. Offers an extensive list of newspapers for parents from all over the U.S. and beyond. These papers are looking for practical information for parents from local sources. For $35 a year, writers can be listed in their database for possible assignments from member newspapers.

Refdesk.com, Refdesk,com/paper.html. Find all the major papers in one place.

Wall Street Journal op-ed guidelines–opinionjournal.com/guidelines.

Washington Post op-ed guidelines–washingtonpost.com/wp-dyn/ content/opinions/index.html.

World Association of Newspapers, wan-press.org. Find links here to English-language newspapers published all over the world.

Worldwide Freelance Writer, worldwidefreelance.com. Here's another place to find markets beyond the United States. Subscribe to their weekly newsletter for market information and helpful articles.

The Writer's and Photographer's Guide to Global Markets, Michael Sedge, Allworth Press. Although this book is a little dated, it offers great information about writing for publications outside the United States.

Writer's Handbook, The Writer Books. Published annually, includes more than sixty articles on freelance writing. Although listings for newspapers are limited, it does offer submission guidelines for the syndicates that sell material such as columns, features and comics to newspapers. Their website, writermag.com, also includes market information.

Writer's Market, Writer's Digest, Inc. Published annually both in paperback and online at writersmarket.com. Lists many magazines open to freelancers. Many libraries have *Writer's Market* in their reference sections. Look for the most recent edition because things change quickly in the publishing business.

Writing-World.com. This site is a great source for all sorts of information for writers. Among the many pages is a list of places to find newspaper guidelines.

Yahoo–dir.yahoo.com/recreation/travel/news_and_media/magazines. A good place to look for travel article markets.

Resources to help you conduct research

Internet Search Engines

As of this writing, Google.com is the most used search engine, but different search engines return different results so if you don't find what you want at one, try another.

ask.com
alltheweb.com

dogpile.com

google.com

metacrawler.com—This search engine searches the other search engines and puts it all together for you.

yahoo.com

Websites to use to access information

Encyclopedia Britannica, britannica.com. The website includes encyclopedia articles and links to other relevant websites and books.

Findarticles.com. This is a gold mine.

Itools.com. This is a dazzling directory of directories.

MagPortal.com. This site offers free access to full-text articles from a variety of magazines.

Newsdirectory.com. Look up articles in newspapers from all over the world here.

Newswise.com. This site provides press releases from the top institutions in scientific, medical, liberal arts and business research. Joining their mailing list is free.

Population Reference Bureau, prb.org. Find lots of helpful statistics here.

The Reference Desk, refdesk.com. This is like going to the library from your home.

Statistical Abstract of the United States, U.S. Department of Commerce, Bureau of the Census. Available online at census.gov/prod/www/statistical-abstract.html, The abstract compiles statistics, including census data, from several government agencies.

WhoWhere?, whowhere.lycos.com. Looking for someone's telephone number or e-mail address? Try here.

Wikipedia.com. A giant, multilingual free-content encyclopedia on the Internet. Great place to start your research.

Places to find experts to interview

Ask an Expert, askanexpert.com. Type in your questions and get referrals to experts who can answer them.

Encyclopedia of Associations, Gale Publishing. This book, updated annually, is a great place to locate sources. Find it in the reference section at the library.

Experts.com. Here's another source of experts who have agreed to answer questions online.

Profnet, profnet.prnewswire.com. Ask a question on this site, and obtain referrals to experts from universities all over the country.

Places to find photographs

Library of Congress, Prints and Photographs Division, loc.gov.

National Archives, Still Picture Branch, archives.gov/research/fromats/photographs-dc.html.

Yahoo Images, images.search.yahoo.com.

Google Images, images.google.com.

Ask Jeeves Pictures, pictures.ask.com.

Picsearch.com.

Shutterstock.com.

The place to find copyright information

Library of Congress, Copyright Office, copyright.gov. This is the place to learn about copyrights. You can download forms to copyright your material online.

Resources to help with word choice

A Writer's Reference by Diana Hacker, Bedford Books. This is a handy book with lots of tabs and tables to help keep you on the straight and narrow and away from clichés like the one I just used.

Bryson's Dictionary of Troublesome Words by Bill Bryson, Broadway Books. Is it *affect* or *effect, premier* or *premiere*? Bryson will tell you.

The Free Dictionary—thefreedictionary.com. This site is amazing. Not only is it a dictionary and thesaurus, but it gives you lots of information about a vast number of topics and tells you more about words than you ever thought to ask.

Resources to help you further your career

American Journalism Review, ajr.org. This site and the magazine that goes with it offer useful information for freelance journalists as well as staff writers and editors.

American Society of Journalists and Authors, asja.org. This organization represents hundreds of independent journalists. Membership is restricted to those with national publication credits or published books, but anyone can read their monthly newsletters and other useful information on their website.

American Society of Newspaper Editors, asne.org. If you're looking for a job at a newspaper or for a contact at any daily or weekly in the United States, you'll probably find it here.

Asian American Journalists Association, aaja.org. This nonprofit professional and educational organization has more than 2,000 members with Asian or Pacific Island roots.

Editor and Publisher. If you want to get a newspaper job, start reading this magazine. For information, visit editorandpublisher.com.

Internet Journalism Resources, mnstate.edu/gunarat/ijr/ journalism.html. This site hosted by Moorhead State University offers links to information sources, newspapers, journalism associations and more.

Journalismjobs.com. Extensive listings of jobs and freelance opportunities in newspapers, magazines, radio, television and online media can be found here.

National Writers Union, nwu.org. The trade union for freelance writers.

Newspaper and Press Associations in the U.S., shgresources.com/ resources/newspapers/associations. Here's a great list of associations for newspaper writers and editors.

Society of Professional Journalists, spj.org. It's a bit costly to join this organization, but a magazine, workshops, a job bank, and career advice are among the benefits for members.

Society of American Travel Writers, satw.org.

Travelwriters.com. This site provides opportunities for writers to connect with editors, PR agencies, and travel-industry professionals.

Books for writers

The Associated Press Stylebook and Briefing on Media Law, Perseus Books. This is the tool that most newspaper editors use to decide how to handle numbers, capitalization, hyphenation, abbreviations and other style matters. It is jammed with fascinating information, and it will help you avoid the little things that drive editors crazy. Look for more information on this at ap.org.

Damn! Why Didn't I Write That? How Ordinary People are Raking in $100,000.00 or More Writing Nonfiction Books & How You Can Too!, Marc McCutcheon, Quill Driver Books. The subtitle of this inspirational book tells it all.

The Elements of Style, William Strunk, Jr., E. B. White, and Roger Angell, Allyn & Bacon. This tiny book is a classic reference on grammar and word usage that should be in every writer's library.

Emotional Structure: Creating the Story Beneath the Plot–A Guide for Screenwriters, Peter Dunne, Quill Driver Books. Read this jewel by three-time Emmy award winner if you are interested in writing for film or television.

The Fast-Track Course on How to Write a Nonfiction Book Proposal, Stephen Blake Mettee, Quill Driver Books. Short and succinct, this guide is used by UCLA and other universities. Recommended by literary agents to those wishing to get a nonfiction book published.

Feminine Wiles: Creative Techniques for Writing Women's Feature Stories that Sell, Donna Elizabeth Boetig, Quill Driver Books. Feature stories written for women are a mainstay of many magazines as well as weekend sections of newspapers.

Freelance Writing for Magazines and Newspapers: Breaking In Without Selling Out, Marcia Yudkin, HarperCollins. Small but mighty, this book will help you get started at freelance writing and keep going. Yudkin also offers advice on the writing business at yudkin.com.

How to Publish Your Articles, Shirley Kawa-Jump, Square One Publishers. This is a great introduction to freelance article writing. The chapters are clearly written, attractively laid out, and full of facts about all kinds of freelancing, including some information about newspapers.

How to Write and Sell a Column, Julie Raskin and Carolyn Males, Writer's Digest Books. The title says it all. Although this book was published pre-Internet, you can still find useful information here.

How to Write Irresistible Query Letters, Lisa Collier Cool, Writer's Digest Books.

LifeWriting: Drawing from Personal Experience to Create Features You Can Publish, Fred D. White, Ph. D., Quill Driver Books. Shows how to write personal-experience narratives drawn from your life or the lives of others.

The New Comedy Writing Step-by-Step: Revised and Updated with Words of Instruction, Encouragement, and Inspiration from Legends of the Comedy Profession, Gene Perret, Quill Driver Books. Written by Bob Hope's chief writer, the original edition was in print for twenty-five years.

Make a Real Living as a Freelance Writer, Jenna Glatzer, Nomad Press. Glatzer tells it like it is. If you're a beginner, this book might scare you out of the business, but if you've been at it for a while, I recommend it.

On Writing Well, William Zinsser, HarperCollins. Teach your words to sing with this wonderful book on writing.

The Portable Writer's Conference: Your Guide to Getting and Staying Published, edited by Stephen Blake Mettee, Quill Driver Books. A writer's conference in a book with "workshops" and "keynotes" written by more than forty-five editors, agents and authors. Ninety percent of what you need to know to get published—the rest you can't learn from a book.

Quit Your Day Job!: How to Sleep Late, Do What You Enjoy, and Make a Ton of Money as a Writer, Jim Denney, Quill Driver Books. Denney does just what the subtitle says and shows you how you can too.

Starting Your Career as a Freelance Writer, Moira Anderson Allen, Allworth Press. If you want to go beyond newspapers, this book will give you a clear path to publication.

Successful Syndication, Michael Sedge, Allworth Press.

Travel Writer's Guide, Gorden Burgett, Communication Unlimited.

Travel Writing, Peat O'Neil, Writer's Digest Books.

The Travel Writer's Handbook: How to Write and Sell Your Own Travel Experiences, Louise Purwin Zobel, Jacqueline Harmon Butler, Surrey Books.

Writers' and Artists' Hideouts: Great Getaways for Seducing the Muse, Andrea Brown, Quill Driver Books. Need some peace and quiet to get your writing started or finished? Here are hundreds of places to escape to, from $19 per night hostels to $1,000 per night luxury spots.

Writer's Guide to Queries, Pitches and Proposals, Moira Anderson Allen, Allworth Press.

You Can Write a Column, Monica McCabe Cardoza, Writer's Digest Books. This is a great guide for starting a column, with lots of exercises to prod you along.

Submission Tracking Sheet
Photocopy this page and use for each item submitted

Title: _____

Notes:

① Publisher: _____ Editor: _____ Phone: _____

Address: _____ Date submitted: _____ Multiple Submission? No Yes

Date to follow up: _____ Date followed up: _____ Follow-up note: _____ Date accepted: _____

Date rejected: _____ Pub date: _____ Payment due date: _____ Payment amount: _____ Clips received: _____

② Publisher: _____ Editor: _____ Phone: _____

Address: _____ Date submitted: _____ Multiple Submission? No Yes

Date to follow up: _____ Date followed up: _____ Follow-up note: _____ Date accepted: _____

Date rejected: _____ Pub date: _____ Payment due date: _____ Payment amount: _____ Clips received: _____

③ Publisher: _____ Editor: _____ Phone: _____

Address: _____ Date submitted: _____ Multiple Submission? No Yes

Date to follow up: _____ Date followed up: _____ Follow-up note: _____ Date accepted: _____

Date rejected: _____ Pub date: _____ Payment due date: _____ Payment amount: _____ Clips received: _____

④ Publisher: _____ Editor: _____ Phone: _____

Address: _____ Date submitted: _____ Multiple Submission? No Yes

Date to follow up: _____ Date followed up: _____ Follow-up note: _____ Date accepted: _____

Date rejected: _____ Pub date: _____ Payment due date: _____ Payment amount: _____ Clips received: _____

⑤ Publisher: _____ Editor: _____ Phone: _____

Address: _____ Date submitted: _____ Multiple Submission? No Yes

Date to follow up: _____ Date followed up: _____ Follow-up note: _____ Date accepted: _____

Date rejected: _____ Pub date: _____ Payment due date: _____ Payment amount: _____ Clips received: _____

The Author's Bundle of Rights

According to United States copyright law, the writer's work is considered copyrighted from the moment it is written. This automatically gives the author ownership of a bundle of rights to his or her work. (Copyright laws differ from country to country so be sure to review and understand your country's copyright laws. In most instances, many of the terms and concepts listed here will still be applicable.)

This bundle of rights may be divided and sold in any number of pieces and with any limitations the author can conceive of and get a publisher to agree to. The writer assigns the right to use the work to publishers, according to the contract between the writer and the publisher.

Many experts suggest that writers list on the manuscript just what rights are being offered. For example, type "First North American Serial Rights" on the upper right hand corner of a short story or article, just above the word count. Always check your contract (or letter of acceptance from the editor) to see what rights the publication expects to receive.

This is just a brief summary of some of the components of the bundle rights. For specific questions, it is always best to consult an attorney who specializes in communications, copyright or publication law.

All rights– Just what it sounds like. When a writer sells "all rights" to a work to a publisher, this means the writer no longer has any say in future publication of the piece. If you want to use it again, say to include a short story in an anthology, you would have to get permission from the publisher to whom you sold the rights. It's always a good idea to avoid selling "all rights," unless the amount offered is very good or the writer decides that the sale–for prestige or another reason–is worth abdicating all rights to the piece.

Electronic rights– This is a term used to define a bundle of rights related to computer technology. It may include the right to reproduce the material on CD-ROMs, in online databases, in multimedia or interactive media, or with publishing-on-demand systems. Just like all other rights, an author may wish to assign certain electronic rights and retain others.

First North American rights– A specific form of first serial rights. This is an agreement to let a periodical use the material for the first time in any periodical within North America. This is the most common type of first rights used in the United States and Canada.

First serial rights– The right to be the first periodical to publish the material. May be limited geographically.

Foreign language rights– The right to reproduce the material in one or more foreign languages. This also may involve geographic limitations.

Foreign rights– These include the right to publish the material outside of the originating country. These may be broken down by country or by some other geographical division such as European rights and may involve foreign language rights.

Onetime rights– This is generally used when a writer sells an article to many noncompeting newspapers or small magazines. This means the periodical buys nonexclusive rights to use the piece once.

Second serial rights– Also called reprint rights. This gives a periodical the chance to print a piece that has already appeared somewhere else. Like onetime rights, these are nonexclusive.

Simultaneous rights– The right to publish the material at the same time; purchased by two or more periodicals. This may be the case with publications with noncompeting markets.

Subsidiary rights– This is a term that refers any secondary rights including, but not limited to,

> Audio rights
> Book club rights
> Character rights
> Condensation rights
> Dramatic rights
> > TV rights
> > Film rights
> Mass-market paperback rights
> Merchandising rights
> Trade paperback rights
> Translation rights

As you can see, these apply mostly to book-length works. A wise author retains as many subsidiary rights as possible or at least makes an agreement for the author to share in any revenue generated by the sale or use of such rights.

Standard Manuscript Format

There is no single correct physical format for a manuscript, but following common format conventions, as shown here, is a good way to say to an editor: "I am a professional." Always use letterhead-sized, white paper. Always be sure the print is dark and legible. Paper clip sheets together or use a manuscript box; never staple.

Author's Name
Street Address
City, State Zip
Phone Number
Social Security Number

Rights Available
Copyright © Year
Approx.: XXXX words

List the rights you're offering to sell.

Some say a copyright notice is the mark of a novice. Most editors won't care either way.

Round word count off to nearest 50 or 100.

Social security number is necessary for government reporting of payments.

TITLE OF ARTICLE, BOOK OR STORY

by Author's Name

Come down about one-third and type the title in all caps. Double space and type "by" and the author's name.

Lorem ipsum dolor sit amet, consectetuer adipiscing elit, sed diam nonummy nibh euismod tincidunt ut laoreet dolore magna aliquam erat volutpat. Ut wisi enim ad minim veniam, quis nostrud exerci tation ullamcorper suscipit lobortis nisl ut aliquip ex ea commodo consequat.

Duis autem vel eum iriure dolor in hendrerit in vulputate velit esse molestie consequat, vel illum dolore eu feugiat nulla facilisis at vero eros et accumsan et iusto odio dignissim qui blandit praesent luptatum zzril delenit augue duis dolore te feugait nulla facilisi.

Lorem ipsum dolor sit amet, consectetuer adipiscing elit, sed diam nonummy nibh euismod tincidunt ut laoreet

Leave four blank lines, then start the text.

Indent paragraphs.

Double space text. Do not right-justify it.

Left, right and bottom margins should be 1"-1½" wide.

Last name/Title/4

Place a slug line: last name /a key word from the title /page number, one-quarter of an inch down, right justified, on all but first page.

Leave 1½" blank at top of sheet.

dolore magna aliquam erat volutpat. Ut wisi enim ad minim veniam, quis nostrud exerci tation ullamcorper suscipit lobortis nisl ut aliquip ex ea commodo consequat. Duis autem vel eum iriure dolor in hendrerit in vulputate velit esse

molestie consequat, vel illum dolore eu feugiat nulla facilisis at.

END

Drop 4 lines below end of text and type "MORE," except on the last page type "-30-" or "END."

Acknowledgments

Portions of this book have previously appeared in:

Byline Magazine: "Prove Your Story with Evidence," Dec. 2004; "When to Stop Writing and Think," Jan. 2004

Writer's Digest: "Tax Relief," published in the April 2006 issue and also in *Writer's Yearbook* 2007.

The Writer: "If I Could Just Make This Call," Aug. 2003.

The Scriptorium online newsletter, my "Everything But Writing" column, March 2005-present, has covered some of the topics included here.

Starting Your Career as a Freelance Writer, Moira Anderson Allen, Allworth Press, 2003, Chapter 15, "Writing for Newspapers."

Writing-World.com: "Newspapers: A Great Source of Freelance Opportunities."

Thank you to Stephen Blake Mettee of Quill Driver Books for seeing the possibilities in this book and guiding me through publication. Special thanks to Moira Allen for helping me to begin this journey by hosting my Freelancing for Newspapers course at writing-world.com. This book began as the lessons I wrote for that course to meet one of the requirements for my MFA degree at Antioch University Los Angeles. I have continued to teach the class online at suelick.com and have taught variations of it at Oregon Coast Community College and at the annual Willamette Writers conference. Thank you to all the students who have allowed me to be their teacher and especially for every question they asked that became part of this book.

Thank you to David L. Ulin, who was my mentor at Antioch University during the spring 2003 semester. He was a tough editor, but made my work so much better. In a program full of literary writers, I knew right away that as newspaper people, we spoke the same language.

I also thank my professors at San Jose State University who got me started in my journalism career and the many editors with whom I have worked over the years. A special thank you to Dolores Spurgeon who has supported my work since I first took her freelancing class in 1973.

In addition, I thank my husband Fred for putting up with the crazy hours and sporadic income of a wife who is always scribbling in her notebook and frequently forgets dinner as she fights to finish one more thing in the office.

Index

About the Author

Sue Fagalde Lick moved from a longtime career as a newspaper reporter, photographer and editor into full-time freelance writing. She has published three books on Portuguese Americans and has sold more articles than she can count to magazines and daily, weekly and specialty newspapers. She earned her BA in journalism from San Jose State University and her MFA in creative nonfiction from Antioch University Los Angeles. She has taught writing workshops at Oregon Coast Community College and online through Writing-world.com. A former president of the South Bay branch of California Writer's Club, she cofounded the Oregon Coast branch of Willamette Writers and is a member of the Willamette Writers board of directors. She and her husband, Fred, live near Newport on the Oregon coast.

To discuss the freelance newspaper business with Sue, visit her blog, freelancingfornewspapers.blogspot.com.

Please visit
QuillDriverBooks.com
for free reports on writing
and to sign up for a free e-newsletter
on writing and getting published.

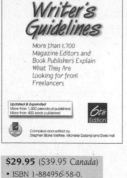
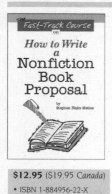